Pathways to African Export Sustainability

Pathways to African Export Sustainability

Paul Brenton, Olivier Cadot, and Martha Denisse Pierola

THE WORLD BANK
Washington, D.C.

Contents

Boxes

Figures

Tables

Acknowledgments

This report was written by Paul Brenton, Olivier Cadot, and Martha Denisse Pierola with assistance from the Bank-Netherlands Partnership Program (BNPP) Trust Fund 092945. The authors are grateful to the Netherlands government for providing the financial resources necessary to carry out background research, including an original survey of African exporters and the collection of data from customs administrations in a number of African countries. We thank the customs authorities in Ghana (Ghana Revenue Authority), Malawi (Malawi Revenue Authority), Mali (Direction Générale des Douanes), Senegal (Direction Générale des Douanes), and Tanzania (Tanzania Revenue Authority) for providing the team with the exporter-level transaction data required to conduct research. We also thank Francis Aidoo, William Baah-Boateng, Caesar Cheelo, Sidiki Guindo, Anthony Mveyange, and Nelson Nsiku for their very valuable efforts supporting the team during the data collection and survey implementation stage of this project. The report is based on background papers by Felix Arndt, Gaelle Balineau, Céline Carrère, Jaime de Melo, Laure Dutoit, Leonardo Iacovone, Julien Gourdon, Mélise Jaud, Marie-Agnès Jouanjean, Madina Kukenova, Jean-Christophe Maur, Marcelo Olarreaga, Caglar Ozden, Ferdinand Rauch, Yuliya Shakurova, and Ben Shepherd. We are particularly grateful for the comments and suggestions of the peer reviewers of this report: Elisa Gamberoni and Javier Suarez.

About the Authors

Paul Brenton is the Trade Practice Leader in the Poverty Reduction and Economic Management Department of the Africa Region of the World Bank. He co-edited the recent World Bank volume on *De-Fragmenting Africa: Deepening Regional Integration in Goods and Services*. Previously he served in the Trade Department of the Bank, where he worked for several years on issues related to trade reform with a focus on regional integration. Dr. Brenton joined the Bank in 2002, having been Senior Research Fellow and Head of the Trade Policy Unit at the Centre for European Policy Studies in Brussels. Before that he was a lecturer in Economics at the University of Birmingham in the United Kingdom. He has a Ph.D. in Economics from the University of East Anglia.

Olivier Cadot is a Professor of International Economics and Director of the Institute of Applied Economics at the University of Lausanne, Switzerland. Prior to taking up his position at Lausanne, he was Associate Professor of Economics at INSEAD. He has held visiting appointments at University of California, Los Angeles (UCLA) and McGill University, New York University, Université d'Auvergne, Koç University, the Paris School of Economics, and the Institut d'Etudes Politiques de Paris. He was a Senior Economist in the World Bank's Trade Department between

2009 and 2011, and has advised the French government, the Swiss federal government, and the European Commission on trade policy matters. He also worked for the Organisation for Economic Co-operation and Development (OECD) and the International Monetary Fund. He was elected best teacher at HEC (Faculty of Business and Economics) Lausanne and was nominated three times for the Outstanding Teacher Award at INSEAD. He has contributed regularly to international executive programs. He is a Research Fellow of the Center for Economic Policy Research in London, a Senior Fellow of the FERDI (Foundation for International Development Study and Research), and Associate Scholar at CEPREMAP (Center for Economic Research and its Applications). He serves on the editorial board of the *Revue d'Economie du Développement* and on the scientific advisory board of the Fondation Jean Monnet. He has published numerous scholarly papers on international trade and economic development. Professor Cadot holds a Ph.D. in Economics from Princeton University and a Master's in Economic History from McGill University.

Martha Denisse Pierola is an Economist in the Trade and International Integration Unit of the Development Research Group of the World Bank. She has published several papers on export growth and exporter dynamics and is currently managing the development of the first-ever global database on exporter growth and dynamics, based on firm-level export data. Previously, she worked on issues related to regionalism, trade costs, and trade and productivity. Before joining the World Bank in 2005, she worked as an economist for the Peruvian government (INDECOPI) and also consulted for the private sector and other international organizations. She has a Ph.D. in Economics from the Graduate Institute of International Studies in Geneva, Switzerland, and a Master's in International Law and Economics from the World Trade Institute in Bern, Switzerland.

Abbreviations

ACP	African, Caribbean, and Pacific
ASEAN	Association of Southeast Asian Nations
ASYCUDA/SYDONIA	Automated System for Customs Data/Système Douanier Automatisé
CACM	Central American Common Market
CMT	cut, make, and trim
COMESA	Common Market for Eastern and Southern Africa
COMTRADE	United Nations Commodity Trade Statistics Database
CPC	crop-protection chemical
DID	difference-in-difference
ECA	Europe and Central Asia
ECOWAS	Economic Community of West African States
EMIC	exporter country migrants in importing country
EPA	Environmental Protection Agency
EU	European Union
EU-REP	Euro-Retailer Produce Working Group

FDA	Food and Drug Administration
FD&C	Food, Drug and Cosmetics Act
FFV	fresh fruit and vegetables
FSIS	Food Safety and Inspection Service
GAP	good agricultural practices
HACCP	hazard analysis and critical control points
HS	Harmonized System
ICM	integrated crop management
IPM	integrated pest management
IT	import tolerance
KM	Kaplan-Meier survivor functions
LAC	Latin America and the Caribbean
LPI	Logistics Performance Index
MENA	Middle East and North Africa
MERCOSUR	*Mercado Común del Sur* (Southern Cone Common Market)
MRL	Maximum Residue Levels
NAFTA	North American Free Trade Agreement
OECD	Organisation for Economic Co-operation and Development
PIP	Pesticide Initiative Program
PPP	Purchasing Power Parity
RASFF	Rapid Alert System for Food and Feed
RFII	Revealed Factor Intensity Indices
ROO	rules of origin
RPED	Regional Program on Enterprise Development
SACU	Southern African Customs Union
SADC	Southern African Development Community
SITC	Standard International Trade Classification
SPS	sanitary and phytosanitary measures
SSA	Sub-Saharan Africa
TFP	total factor productivity
UAE	United Arab Emirates
UEMOA	Union Economique et Monétaire Ouest Africaine (West African Economic and Monetary Union)
UN	United Nations
UNCTAD	United Nations Conference on Trade and Development
U.S.	United States

Introduction

African exporters suffer from low survival in international markets. This means that they fail more often than other exporters, undermining their reputation with foreign buyers and condemning themselves to incurring again and again the setup costs involved in starting new relationships. This high churning is a source of waste, uncertainty, and discouragement. Can something be done about it?

Is this really the case? The paragraph above had the pessimistic overtone of most of the literature on African economic performance, whether on export markets or otherwise. But does this pessimism withstand scrutiny? This report will show that the answer is "no." When survival performance is controlled for by observable country characteristics such as—among other things—the level of income, Africa is no outlier. African exports have short life expectancies, but not any shorter than comparable countries. Beyond income levels, short export survival is largely explained by the difficult business environment in which African exporters operate. Once measures of this environment are taken into account, African countries are by no means "below the regression line" in terms of export survival.

There is more to dispel the dismal tone of our opening paragraph. African exporters, like those in other low-income countries, show extraordinarily vigorous entrepreneurship. Entry rates into new products and new markets are high in spite of the formidable hurdles created by poor infrastructure and landlockedness for some or limited access to major sea routes for others. African exporters experiment a lot, and frequent failure is a price to pay for a chance to succeed. In fact, it is the basic mechanism through which populations improve, through what biologists call "Darwinism" and economists call "creative destruction." In that sense, low survival is good news.

Why should we worry, then? We should be concerned about low export survival for the same reason we are concerned with high infant mortality. Every failure has a cost, and the very high failure rates that we observe suggest, beyond experimentation, that the environment must be so rough that it is bound to entail a large proportion of "accidental" deaths. It is those deaths that we want to reduce through better policies.

Lessons from empirical evidence gathered in background papers to this report and from a recent survey of African exporters carried out by the World Bank, also as background to this report, suggest that the environment in which African exporters operate can be improved through traditional prescriptions to improve trade facilitation, the legal environment of business, better access to credit, and also through more proactive interventions targeting the firms themselves, provided that those interventions are well designed.

This report provides tentative leads toward such policy prescriptions, based on an overview of the empirical evidence. Chapter 1 sets the stage by putting Africa's export-survival performance into perspective and proposing a framework that will guide the interpretation of empirical evidence throughout the report. Chapter 2 covers country-level determinants of export sustainability at origin and destination, including the exporting country's business environment. Chapter 3 explores some of the firm-level evidence on what drives export sustainability, including uncertainty, incomplete contracts, learning, and networks. Finally, chapter 4 offers tentative policy implications.

The main conclusions from this overview of the causes of Africa's low export sustainability should be taken with caution both because of the complexity of the issue and because of the very fragmentary evidence on which the overview is based. We should be more cautious in drawing policy implications, as hasty policy prescriptions are the most common trap into which reports of this kind can fall. A first, solid conclusion is that we need substantial additional work on the nature and causes of low export survival rates in developing countries to determine the path to high export sustainability. We close the report with some suggestions of where new work is most needed.

Yet, before that, we do propose a number of additional tentative remarks linking this work with recent analysis on barriers to trade in Africa presented in the World Bank report *De-Fragmenting Africa: Deepening Regional Trade Integration in Goods and Services* (http://go. worldbank.org/MKK5U1Y2D0). First, Africa suffers from a low-survival syndrome because its business environment is a difficult one. Trade costs are high, directly—because of high freight rates and long inland routes; and indirectly—because of burdensome customs and administrative procedures and substantial non-tariff barriers. Productive capacities are constrained by many factors, prominent among which is the lack of access to critical services, including credit from financial services providers, which prevents African exporters from responding in time to escalating buyer demands.

As a result of this difficult environment, Africa may find it difficult to nurture the kind of midsize exporters that have proved, in other environments, to be the most adaptable and resilient to changing competitive situations. Because of the continent's small and fragmented domestic markets and low levels of intra-regional trade, African exporters have little opportunity to gain local experience before being approached by larger buyers, often resulting in mismatch and premature failure.

However, there are grounds to be optimistic. Intra-regional trade is growing but remains a small fraction of its potential. Although tariff barriers have been reduced or removed in many regional communities in Africa, non-tariff barriers remain a major constraint to trade in goods while limits on market access and restrictive regulatory regimes limit trade in services. While still a major issue, the infrastructure deficit in Africa is coming down—but here it is important to coordinate investments in infrastructure with policy reforms that deliver competitive services. In addition, as African diasporas abroad gain in economic status, they are posited to help the continent's exporters reach out to new markets with which they have little familiarity, like other—especially Asian— diasporas have long done for their home countries.

Governments can help secure and accelerate these positive trends. They can help, first, by vigorously pursuing trade-facilitation agendas and by working to improve the business environment in which exporters operate. They can also work to improve the performance of export-promotion agencies with a view toward better sustainability of results and more strategic assistance on optimal long-term export-expansion paths.

Efforts to promote the deeper integration of African markets through more effective regional agreements will help African exporters accumulate experience on markets with which they can rapidly gain familiarity and where consumers have similar preferences. These efforts should focus on providing transparent, predictable, and stable trade policy environments and avoid abrupt changes in non-tariff barriers as a response to temporary market disruptions or to lobbying demands. They should also target the simplification and relaxation of rules of origin so as to foster the emergence of regional supply chains populated by firms of similar size and outlook, as this has been shown in other contexts to be a factor in long-lasting relationships.

Finally, African countries and international organizations should engage in dialogue with industrial countries to reduce the current degree of discretionarity in the application of sanitary and phytosanitary standards for agri-food products, as is current practice in some Organisation for Economic Co-operation and Development countries, based on reputation as much as evidence. This tends to penalize new exporters with no established records, creating uncertainty through a constant risk of rejection.

Since this is an early report in the analysis of export survival in Africa, there is clearly much scope and need for further research. The following are a number of areas that stand out for additional analysis:

- There is a need to understand the role of export intermediaries. For a number of products, especially raw agricultural products, exports are not undertaken by firms that produce products but rather by export agents that sell overseas the output of a large number of smallholder producers. These intermediaries may be making strategic decisions on where to sell such produce according to prices in particular markets. As such, they may shift exports from one market to another in a way that suggests regular entry and exit from particular markets in the customs statistics.

- The analysis thus far has used official customs statistics and information from firms that are exporting officially. A vast number of traders in Africa operate in the informal sector, in large part because of the hostile business environment and the high costs of formally crossing borders. Part of the pathway to export sustainability will be to facilitate the movement of exporters from the informal to the formal sector, an effort that will have to include addressing the key factors that may undermine their survival as formal exporters. Identifying success stories of exporters that have successfully migrated from the informal to the formal arena can provide important information in this regard.

- The analysis here has focused entirely on trade in goods. An increasingly important feature of the global economy and regional markets in Africa is trade in services. Trade in services holds enormous potential for regional integration in Africa, especially for landlocked countries whose opportunities to trade in manufactures are limited relative to large coastal countries. It would be very useful to look at the survival rates of services flows across borders and their determinants and to see if and how they differ significantly from the situation regarding the survival of goods exports flows.

- More studies are needed that carefully assess the impact of trade promotion and other efforts to encourage exporters, and to include in the analysis not only the impact on export volumes but also on the survival rates of the underlying export firms. Of particular use would be studies looking at impacts of programs that have supported greater participation in regional trade on the subsequent entry of beneficiary firms into global markets.

CHAPTER 1

Export Survival

What We Know about Africa

Recent evidence suggests that export survival is, on average, very low—less than ten years for virtually all trade relationships and around one to two years for the majority of them. It also varies systemically across both origins and destinations, with an apparently strong association with income levels. Is Africa an outlier? A first pass at the evidence suggests a negative answer. Most African export spells fail to survive past one or two years, not because there is something unique to Africa, but because the vast majority of African countries are low-income ones. Why is it that low-income country exports do not survive as well as exports from high-income countries? This report will systematically explore a range of conjectures in this regard.

In this first chapter, we will content ourselves with one simple observation: exporters in low-income countries experiment a great deal, and experimentation is associated with failure as much as with success. To draw an analogy to population dynamics, export markets are characterized by high infant (newcomer) mortality. Low-income countries are characterized by high export birth rates (an active "extensive margin," in the trade jargon). Therefore, they also have high export death rates. The association between high rates of experimentation and high rates of failure reflects a sort of Darwinism—what Joseph Schumpeter called "creative destruction"—and it may well be a healthy process.

However, the infant mortality of exports may be higher in low-income countries for a different reason—namely, because the environment for business generally is too tough. In order to reduce the incidence of "accidental deaths," we need to understand, at least in a basic manner, the logic of exit decisions at the firm level. This is the second objective of this chapter.

Export Survival: A First Pass at the Evidence

In this section, we address survival of export flows by product and destinations. The term *export survival* is basically defined as follows, with slight variants. Consider exports of a given product, say, "linens for the bed, table, toilet and kitchen"—code 6584 in the Standard International Trade Classification (SITC) nomenclature[1]—from Pakistan to Japan. Suppose that no bilateral trade in that product between those two countries was recorded in available trade data until 1985. Starting in 1985, positive flows are observed during, say, five years in a row, followed by an interruption of at least one year. We call this uninterrupted period a *spell*. That is, a *spell* is a product-origin-destination combination for which we observe nonzero trade values for a number of consecutive years. When flows stop, the spell is said to "die." Its duration is the number of years during which we observe positive flows, which in this case is just five years. By *export survival* we mean the average duration of export spells.[2]

Export spells may have multiple lives. That is, exports of SITC 6584 from Pakistan to Japan may stop for a year and then start again. The interruption may be genuine, either because firms that were active during the initial spell decided to exit the "market" (meaning the product-destination combination) and new ones entered a few years later, or because a single firm goes through a period (a "dry spell") with no orders in the market. At the firm level, this may be frequent for durable goods for which orders tend to be bulky. Alternatively, an apparent interruption of a bilateral trade flow may simply be a recording error at customs.[3] In the absence of information beyond trade statistics, the way temporary zero-trade periods should be interpreted is a matter of judgment. Throughout this report, unless indicated otherwise, we will define a *spell death* as an interruption of one year or more. The results we report for a spell death are largely the same as the results of a two-year interruption.

By and large, export survival is low. Besedes and Prusa (2006a, b) were the first to study systematically the survival of export spells at a disaggregated level. Using U.S. import data at the SITC 4-digit level, they found, strikingly, that the average spell duration was 4.4 years, with a median of 2 years, over the 1989–2001 period.[4] Part of the reason for the short average and median survival of export spells is that the majority of them are small in value, and, as we will document in this report, small-value spells are less enduring. When individual spells are weighted (by the square root of their initial value), the weighted-average survival rises to 10.8 years.[5] Brenton, Saborowski, and von Uexkull (2010); Fugazza and Molina (2011); and Subsequent studies by (among others) Nitsch (2009) largely confirmed their findings on increasingly disaggregated data sets. The most comprehensive data set in the literature has been compiled by Carrère and Strauss-Kahn (2011) and yields largely similar results.

Beyond averages, there is substantial heterogeneity across countries at both origin and destination. Figure 1.1 shows that exports originating from Sub-Saharan Africa survive, on average, just over two years, the lowest regional average. Only the Middle East and North Africa comes close to Sub-Saharan Africa in terms of short survival, followed by Latin America and the Caribbean. What this means practically is that, whereas an average exporter in the United States faces a 70 percent probability of surviving beyond the first year in a given product-destination pair, that

Figure 1.1   Average Export Survival by Origin Country, 1979–2010

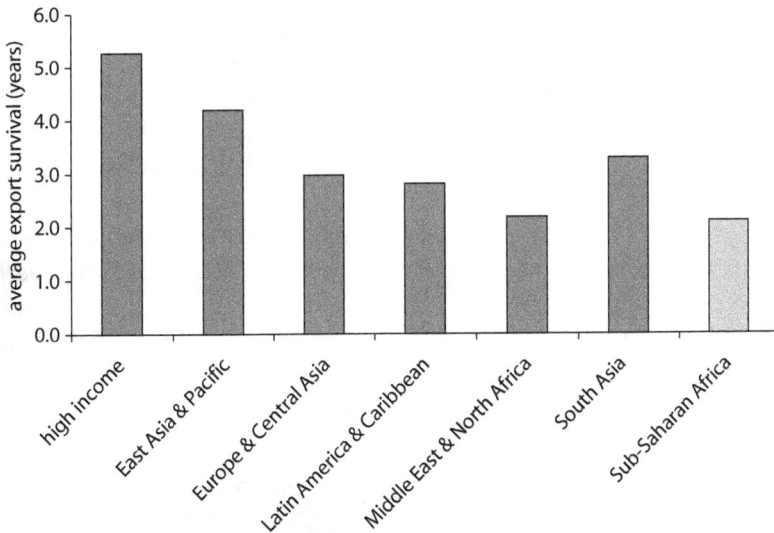

Source: Authors' calculations based on UN Commodity Trade Statistics database.
Note: Average export-spell duration is calculated as the simple average of the duration of all SITC-4 spells to the destinations in the group.

Figure 1.2   Average Export Survival by Destination, 1979–2010

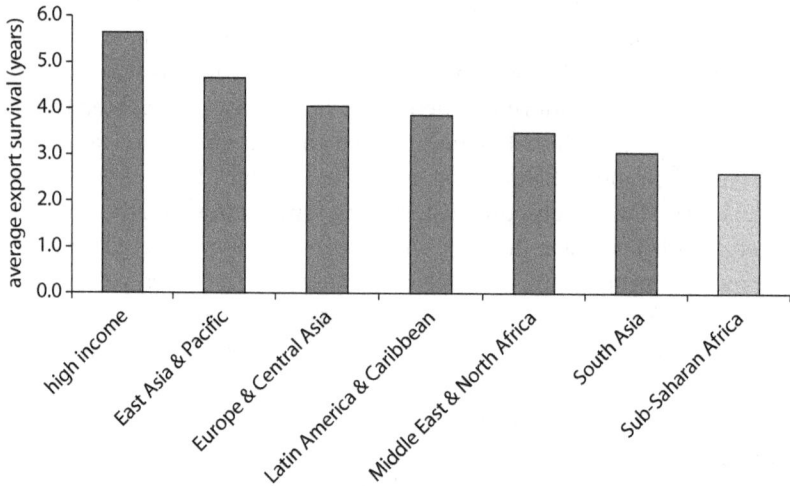

Source: Authors' calculations based on UN Commodity Trade Statistics Trade database.

probability is less than 30 percent for an exporter in Burkina Faso (Brenton et al. 2009).

Survival also varies by destination market, and again Sub-Saharan Africa stands out for its low average survival, as shown in figure 1.2. However, the ranking is slightly different, with South Asia now coming next to Sub-Saharan Africa in terms of low survival, and only then the Middle East and North Africa.

Thus, in a crude comparison by regions, Sub-Saharan Africa stands out at both ends for its low survival, suggesting a tough business environment, prone to failure and sudden interruption, for both exporters and importers. Should this be construed as implying that there is a specifically Sub-Saharan African syndrome of low export survival? Clearly, it is too early to jump to such a conclusion. The crude comparisons shown in figures 1.1 and 1.2 do not control for any covariates—country characteristics such as low income that apply to many countries in Sub-Saharan Africa and that also correlate with low export survival.

Do African Exports Really Survive Less Long?

Based on the evidence presented above, in this section we explore whether Africa—mainly we refer to Sub-Saharan Africa—stands out as an outlier in terms of low export survival.

Setting the Stage: Africa's Export Recovery

After two decades of steep decline, Sub-Saharan Africa exports as a share of global trade bottomed out in the early 2000s and have subsequently been on the rise. In dollar terms, Africa's exports per capita have risen at an annual rate of 13 percent between 1994 and 2008, compared with 4 percent for the United States, 8 percent for Germany, 13 percent for India, and 19 percent for China (Easterly and Resheff 2010). Figure 1.3 shows the turning point by plotting the ratio of Sub-Saharan Africa's non-commodity exports relative to a comparator group made of low-income countries and lower-middle-income countries (excluding those in Sub-Saharan Africa) after eliminating India and China. A clear break in the trend appears just before 2000, although the recovery is still far from offsetting the previous two disastrous decades.

As is often noted, Africa trades little with itself, at least to the extent that is recorded in official customs statistics. There has been a modest increase in the share of total goods exports from Sub-Saharan Africa going to other Sub-Saharan Africa countries, from 11 percent in 1994 to 16 percent in

Figure 1.3   Sub-Saharan Africa's Exports Relative to Comparator Group, 1960–2010

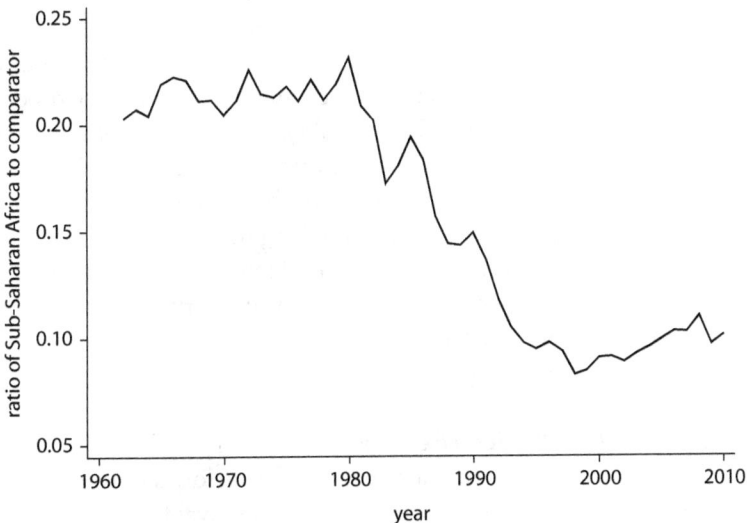

Source: Authors' calculations based on UN Commodity Trade Statistics database.
Note: The comparator group is the set of low-income and lower-middle-income countries excluding India and China—whose size make them noncomparable to any African country—and the line represents the ratio of Sub-Saharan total exports (intra- and extra-African) to the exports of the comparator group. Petroleum and ores are excluded from the total.

2008 (12 percent to 21 percent of non-fuel exports). Trade within regional communities is even lower. For example, the share of intra-regional goods trade in total goods imports is only around 5 percent in the Common Market for Eastern and Southern Africa (COMESA), 10 percent in the Economic Community of West African States (ECOWAS), and 8 percent in the West African Economic and Monetary Union (UEMOA). This compares with over 20 percent in the Association of Southeast Asian Nations (ASEAN), around 35 percent in the North American Free Trade Agreement (NAFTA), and more than 60 percent in the European Union (EU). On the other hand, intra-regional trade in the Southern Cone Common Market (MERCOSUR) is about 15 percent of total imports and less than 8 percent in the Central American Common Market (CACM)—see Acharya et al. (2011). There are, however, substantial informal flows of goods and people across borders in Africa that are not measured in official statistics.

Although exports have grown strongly over the last decade, and even though the region's trade has recovered well from the global crisis, the impact of this recovery on unemployment and poverty has been disappointing in many countries. Unemployment remains around 24 percent in South Africa. In Tanzania, the percentage of people living in extreme poverty (less than US$1.25 a day) appears to have remained broadly constant—around 35 percent of the population. In Burkina Faso, income poverty has been stagnant since 1997. This is because export growth has typically been fueled by a small number of mineral and primary products with limited impact on the wider economy, and because formal sectors remain small in many countries, such as Burkina Faso. Hence, key objectives in Africa remain to diversify the export base away from dependence on commodities and to build on the increasing number of export success stories, thus allowing more people to participate in trade. Therefore, for this study, a key issue is whether increased export survival rates in Africa would not only support sustained export growth but also lead to a more diversified and inclusive export structure.

Export Survival: An "African Exception"?
We saw that Sub-Saharan Africa stands out for its low survival as both a source and a destination of exports. Is this low survival truly a specifically Sub-Saharan African characteristic? We cannot answer this question before controlling for other determinants of export survival. This will be the object of much of this study, but we start with the most obvious suspect—income levels.

Average export survival varies substantially with the level of income of the exporting country, as shown in figure 1.4. At 5.8 years, exports from high-income countries survive, on average, 3.1 times longer than exports from low-income countries (1.8 years). This wide difference suggests a high-risk business environment for low-income exporters, where trade relationships frequently terminate early. Many factors play a role in this environment of short-term relationships, including, as we will see later in this chapter, intensive experimentation by export entrepreneurs in low-income countries.

Figure 1.5 shows that average survival is also, at 6.3 years, 2.7 times higher in high-income markets than in low-income ones (2.3 years) at the destination point, although the relationship is non-monotone, with relatively lower survival observed in high-income countries that are not part of the Organisation for Economic Co-operation and Development (OECD).[6] High survival in higher-income markets is not directly intuitive, as those markets may be tougher in terms of number of competitors, whereas low-income markets—especially in Sub-Saharan Africa—are sometimes sheltered from competition by high trade and transport costs. One countervailing force may be the prevalence of contractual relationships on more structured and sophisticated markets.

More seriously, figure 1.5 does not control for origin countries, and this may introduce a confounding composition effect. A larger fraction of

Figure 1.4   Average Export Survival by Exporter (Origin) Income, 1979–2010

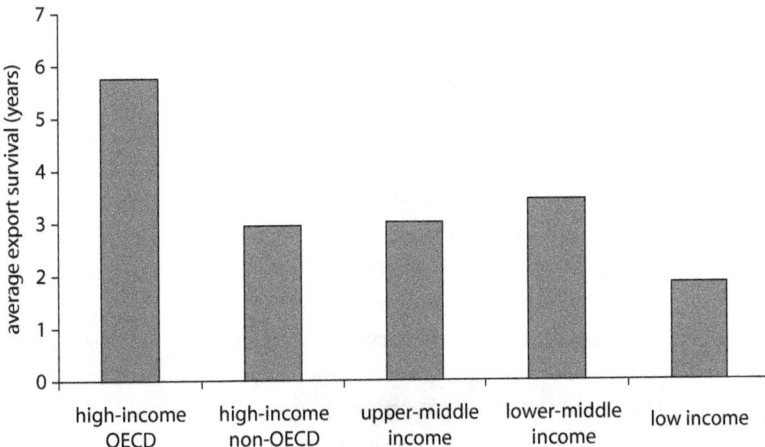

Source: Authors' calculations based on UN Commodity Trade Statistics database.

Figure 1.5   Average Spell Survival by Importer (Destination) Income, 1979–2010

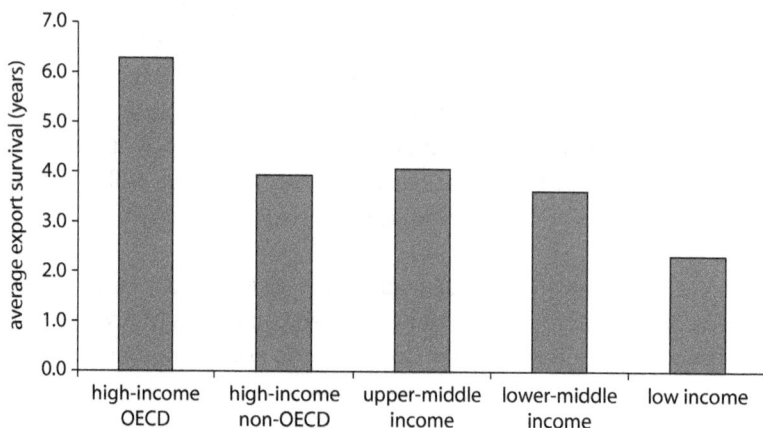

Source: Authors' calculations based on UN Commodity Trade Statistics database.

exports sold in high-income countries originate from high-income origin countries, and we know that exports from high-income origins survive better. Therefore, we cannot tell if the higher survival observed in high-income destination markets reflects their intrinsic characteristics or, instead, the composition of their suppliers. The same observation applies to the variation of survival across origin countries shown in figure 1.4: the variation may well be a reflection of variations in destination portfolios rather than the intrinsic characteristics of origin countries.

A different look at the data is displayed in figure 1.6, which shows Kaplan-Meier (KM) survivor functions. Annex 1B provides a brief explanation of these functions; suffice it to note here that KM survivor functions plot the proportion of individuals (export flows) still alive as a function of time since birth (or onset of risk). As the proportion falls to less than 0.5 after the first year for all three income categories of developing countries (upper-middle-income, lower-middle-income, and low-income countries), the median survival length is just below one year.

Unlike figure 1.4, figure 1.6 controls, albeit coarsely, for destination effects (all spells have OECD countries as destinations). In spite of this control, it is apparent that spell survival is everywhere lower for low-income countries than it is for lower- and upper-middle-income ones, confirming survival's dependence on origin-country income.

Figure 1.7 shows the same function for export spells originating from Sub-Saharan Africa compared with those of other developing countries.

Figure 1.6   Kaplan-Meier Survival Function for Developing-Country Originating Products in OECD Markets

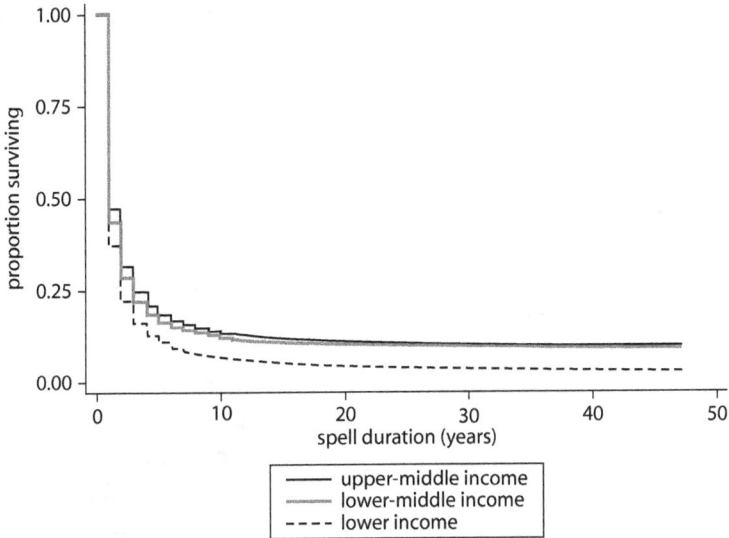

Source: Carrère and Strauss-Kahn 2011, Figure A1.

Figure 1.7   Kaplan-Meier Survival Function for Sub-Saharan Africa–Originating Products in OECD Markets

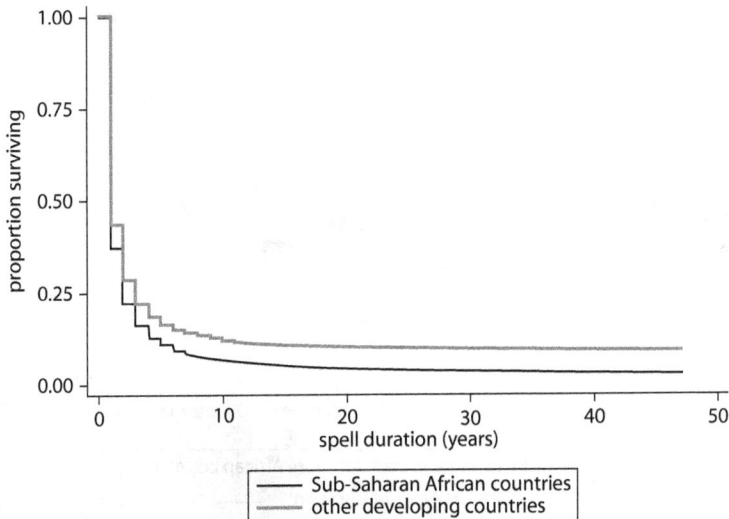

Source: Carrère and Strauss-Kahn 2011, Figure A1.
Note: See annex 1B of this chapter for an explanation of Kaplan-Meier functions.

It is apparent that Sub-Saharan Africa–originating spells are shorter-lived than others.

The pattern of variation apparent in figures 1.4, 1.5, and 1.6 suggests that export spell survival correlates with income. Does this hold up to scrutiny? Figure 1.8, a scatter plot of average spell survival against exporter-country income, together with a quadratic regression curve, provides an interesting answer. The pattern that emerges is non-monotone, with a slight *decrease* up to about US$1,600 purchasing power parity (PPP) and progression at an increasing rate thereafter. Thus, for low-income countries, income rises may not be associated with immediate, "mechanical" increases in average export survival, although there is nothing here to suggest the direction of causality between income and average export survival rates or the factors that can propel both.

Figure 1.8 also shows that once income levels are controlled for, Africa is no outlier. In fact, most Sub-Saharan African countries are bunched around the regression curve. The picture does not change significantly when disaggregated by broad sectors, as shown by figure 1.9.

Thus, as a first pass there does not seem to be an African specificity in terms of low export survival. However, the scatter plots in figures 1.8 and 1.9

Figure 1.8   Average Spell Survival and Exporter-Country Income, 1979–2010

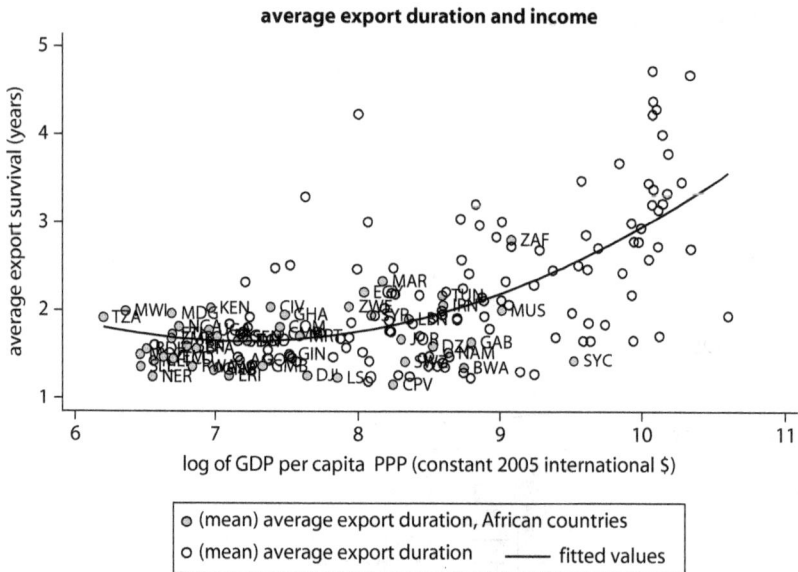

average export duration and income

(y-axis) average export survival (years)

(x-axis) log of GDP per capita PPP (constant 2005 international $)

o (mean) average export duration, African countries

o (mean) average export duration   —— fitted values

Sources: For survival data, authors' calculations based on UN Commodity Trade Statistics database; for GDP per capita, World Development Indicators.
Note: PPP = purchasing power parity

Figure 1.9   Export Survival and Income by Sector, 1979–2010

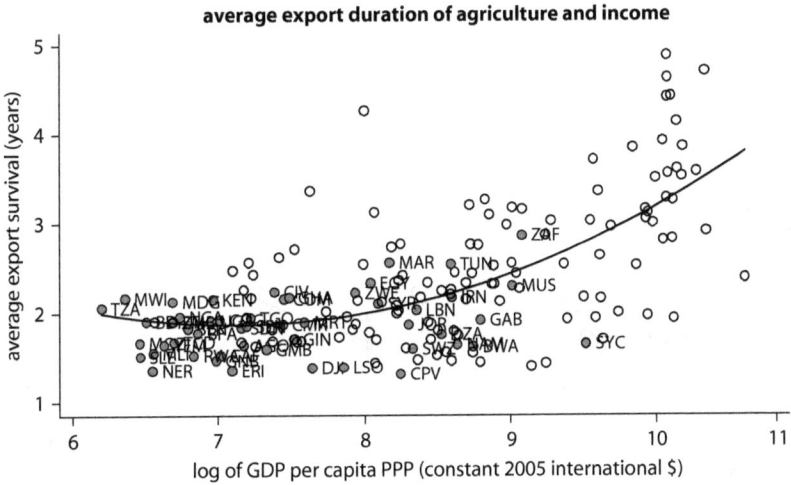

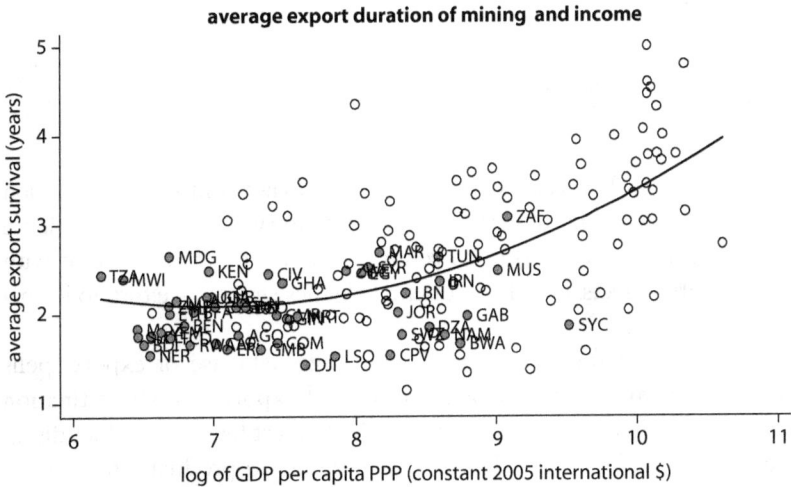

average export duration of agriculture and income

average export duration of mining and income

● (mean) average export duration, African countries ○ (mean) average export duration
——— fitted values

(continued next page)

Figure 1.9 *(continued)*

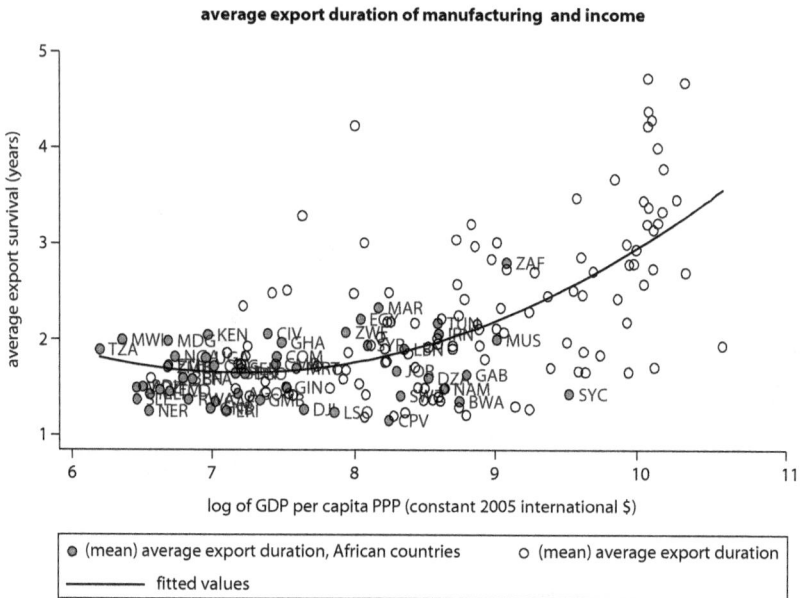

average export duration of manufacturing and income

Sources: For survival data, authors' calculations based on UN Commodity Trade Statistics database; for GDP per capita, World Development Indicators.
Note: PPP = purchasing power parity

can be misleading because, like figure 1.4, they do not control for destination effects. The dependence of survival on origin-country income shown in figure 1.8 may, again, reflect a portfolio-composition effect and confound it with origin-country effects. In order to disentangle these effects, we turn to formal regression analysis.

We assembled for this report a very large database of export spells originating from all developing countries and exported to all destination markets, including OECD countries, at the highest level of product disaggregation (4- and 5-digit SITC, or over a thousand products) from 1979 to 2009. Mirror trade-flow data were used to improve accuracy.[7] Aggregating the trade-flow data into export spells reduced the data's dimensionality somewhat, but left more than 5 million observations. Left-censoring substantially reduced the number of observations. See annex 1B for a brief discussion of technical issues arising from the existence of left-censored spells.

A common tool for the causal analysis of survival is a Cox regression, which uses a maximum-likelihood estimator of hazard rates. We ran a series of Cox regressions of export-spell hazard rates on bilateral, regional, and country-level covariates; these suggest a different picture. Results are shown in table 1.1 in the form of coefficients (not hazard ratios) with z-statistics in parentheses, which can be interpreted like t-statistics (see annex 1B for more explanation of the Cox regression and its interpretation).

Table 1.1   Cox Regression Results: Estimation of Export Spell Hazard Rates, All Developing Countries

	(1)	(2)	(3)	(4)
Spell attributes				
Initial spell value	−0.0617***	−0.0623***	−0.0634***	−0.0634***
	(0.00123)	(0.0012535)	(0.00123)	(0.0012)
Spell value growth	2.4e−08**	2.35e−08**	1.71e−08*	1.71e−08*
	(9.68e−09)	(9.66e−09)	(9.67e−09)	(9.67e−09)
Multiple spell	0.6774***	0.6763***	0.6827***	0.6821***
	(0.00790)	(0.00796)	(0.0077)	(0.0077)
Gravity variables				
ln exporter GDP/cap *		0.0035***		0.0005***
ln importer GDP		(0.00013)		(0.0002)
ln exporter GDP/cap	−0.427***		−0.4523***	
	(0.01824)		(0.0199)	
ln exporter GDP/cap^2	0.026***		0.0271***	
	(0.00101)		(0.0011)	
ln importer GDP/cap	0.0368**		0.0138	
	(0.01679)		(0.0168)	
ln importer GDP/cap^2	−0.0018*		−0.0023**	
	(0.00095)		(0.00095)	
Landlocked exporter	0.1126***	0.1481***	0.1565***	0.1974***
	(0.00794)	(0.0084)	(0.0083)	(0.0089)
Landlocked importer	0.0332***	0.0384***	0.0305***	0.0343***
	(0.00282)	(0.00276)	(0.0026)	(0.0028)
Common border	−0.1222***	−0.1199***	−0.0928***	−0.0872***
	(0.00418)	(0.0043)	(0.004)	(0.004)
Common language	0.0174***	0.0244***	0.0071***	0.006**
	(0.00319)	(0.0032)	(2.64e−03)	(0.0027)
Common colonial past	0.008*	0.0036	0.0107**	*0.0002
	(0.00454)	(0.0046)	(0.0052)	(0.0052)
ln distance	0.0301***	0.0231***	0.0643***	0.0615***
	(0.00179)	(0.0018)	(0.0021)	(0.0021)
Exchange-rate volatility	9.5e−05***	−0.00007***	−0.0001***	−8.3e−05***
	(4.94e−06)	(0.0000)	(5.08e−06)	(0.0000)
ln export cost	0.3918***	0.3412***	0.2721***	0.2303***
	(0.00516)	(0.0047)	(0.0059)	(0.0053)

(continued next page)

Table 1.1 *(continued)*

	(1)	(2)	(3)	(4)
Exporter regional dummies				
Europe and Central Asia		0.2***		0.2***
		(0.0092)		(0.0092)
Latin America & the Caribbean		0.2098***		0.208***
		(0.0071)		(0.0068)
Middle East & North Africa		0.2623***		0.2926***
		(0.008)		(0.0075)
South Asia		−0.0428***		−0.0303***
		(0.0067)		(0.0067)
Sub-Saharan Africa		0.2***		0.2217***
		(0.0077)		(0.0076)
Importer regional dummies				
Europe and Central Asia		−0.0201***		−0.0281***
		(0.0063)		(0.0062)
Latin America & the Caribbean		−0.0399***		−0.0364***
		(0.0051)		(0.0051)
Middle East & North Africa		0.1292***		0.12***
		(0.0055)		(0.0053)
North America		−0.0937***		−0.14***
		(0.0053)		(0.006)
South Asia		−0.1552***		−0.0972***
		(0.006)		(0.0071)
Sub-Saharan Africa		−0.0825***		−0.0414***
		(0.0049)		(0.0057)
Western Europe		0.0501***		0.0134**
		(0.0054)		(0.0055)
Observations	2,457,227	2,457,227	2,450,944	2,450,944
Exporting region FE	no	no	yes	yes
Importing region FE	no	no	yes	yes

Source: Authors' estimations.
Note: Sub-Saharan African values are highlighted with a gray band. Robust standard errors in parentheses.
FE = fixed effects.
*** $p < 0.01$, ** $p < 0.05$, * $p < 0.1$.

Following the logic of the basics of survival explained in annex 1A, we included a number of gravity-type country-pair covariates in the regression (common border, common language, common colonial past, distance) as well as country-level covariates (GDP per capita, landlockedness, trade costs, exchange-rate volatility) and spell covariates (initial value,

value growth, multiple spells) in columns 1 and 2. Then we added exporter-region and importer-region dummies in columns 3 and 4, as well as initial-year time effects (not reported).

The initial spell value correlates negatively with the hazard rate, implying that larger spells tend to survive longer. This is a common finding in the export-survival literature. The positive correlation of hazard rates with spell growth is unintuitive, and it is estimated fairly imprecisely, being significant at the 10 percent level only in some specifications. The positive effect of multiple spells can be interpreted as reflecting the fact that multiple spells and short duration are both reflections of a stop-go pattern in bilateral trade flows.

Results on gravity variables are in line with the predictions of the simple model in annex 1A. Exporter income levels have a non-monotone effect on hazard rates (as importer income levels do), although the shape is, after controlling for other covariates, different from that shown in figure 1.8. Landlockedness raises hazard rates on both the exporter and importer sides, possibly reflecting both higher costs and more frequent disruption of land routes. A common border reduces hazard rates, as it is likely to reflect lower *variable* costs; by contrast, a common language correlates with higher hazard rates, as it is likely to reflect lower *sunk* costs of entry and exit. Colonial past is largely insignificant, whereas distance and export costs correlate positively with hazard rates. Exchange-rate volatility correlates positively with hazard rates when exporter size and importer size are controlled for separately, reflecting the "good-news principle" highlighted in annex 1A.

The second part of the table shows that, interestingly, regional effects remain significant, even after controlling for spell-specific, bilateral, and country-level covariates. The coefficients on regional dummies reflect differential hazard rates compared with those of East Asia and the Pacific, the omitted region.

On the importer side (bottom panel), the Western Europe effect correlates positively with hazard rates, possibly reflecting exporter uncertainty with respect to compliance with standards and other technical issues. We will return to this issue in chapter 3. All other regions have negative specific effects, suggesting that survival in East Asian markets is among the toughest to achieve.

On the exporter side, all except South Asia have higher hazard rates than those of the omitted category, which is East Asia. The strongest regional effect is for the Middle East and North Africa region, followed by Sub-Saharan Africa and Latin America and the Caribbean. Thus, the intuition of figure 1.8 is largely confirmed in the sense that, even though regional specificities do exist, Sub-Saharan Africa is no outlier. Sub-Saharan Africa suffers from a low-survival syndrome that is not entirely explained by the usual covariates, and that does not set it apart from other regions of the world either; in other words, lessons from other continents on both barriers and policy options to overcome them may well be relevant to Sub-Saharan Africa as well.

Understanding Entry, Exit, and Survival Decisions

In this section, we move beyond the trade-flow analysis of export survival and discuss the considerations surrounding survival decisions from a firm's perspective. Entry, exit, and survival decisions are logically related through the interplay of expected returns to the export business, fixed costs, sunk costs, and uncertainty.

Hysteresis and Sunk Costs

The expected return from exporting is derived from additional sales revenue, net of variable and fixed costs; possibly, also, from the indirect effect on other costs—through economies of scale, learning, and so on. It is affected positively by the price of export sales, and negatively by variable and fixed costs of production and distribution. Sunk costs arise when selling abroad involves setting up distribution networks or investing in initial advertising campaigns whose costs cannot be recovered. Uncertainty arises from a number of factors, including fluctuations in the exchange rate, sudden changes in border taxes and non-tariff barriers, or unanticipated changes in transport and marketing costs.

If there were no sunk costs of entry or exit, firms would enter export markets as soon as returns, net of fixed costs, were positive, and exit as soon as they turned negative, producing rapid churning and almost zero survival. Yet this is not exactly what we observe. At the macro level, import flows display what physicists call *hysteresis*—a phenomenon by which temporary shocks have permanent effects. For instance, the temporary dollar overvaluation of the 1980s led to permanent changes in U.S. market structure, as foreign firms established "beachheads" at a time when sales in the United States were hugely profitable, and stayed instead of packing up and going when the dollar fell back down to its long-run value (Baldwin 1988; Baldwin and Krugman 1989; Krugman 1986). At the micro level, we do observe rapid churning, but survival rates vary and are certainly not zero.

To better grasp the issues, annex 1A lays out a simple setup combining uncertainty with fixed and sunk costs. Consider the following situation. A firm is faced with, say, exchange-rate uncertainty in a foreign market where it exports. When the exchange rate is high, it makes money. When it falls, it loses money. If entry and exit were costless, the firm would exit as soon as the exchange rate fell below the breakeven point. But in the presence of sunk costs of reentry, "toughing it out" in bad times has an option value. Annex 1A shows that this option value is (1) increasing with sunk costs of reentry and (2) decreasing in export operating costs. Thus, given an initial situation where the firm is "in," there is a minimum value of the exchange rate at which it decides to exit—that is, to exercise the option. The lower this value, the larger the range of exchange-rate fluctuations within which the firm stays in the export market, which, in turn, implies a longer survival of export spells.

The reasoning is illustrated in figure 1.10. Consider first the left-hand side of the diagram. The sunk cost of reentry S is measured on the left-hand side of the horizontal axis, increasing to the left, and the cutoff value of the exchange rate below which the firm decides to exit export markets, e^{min}, is measured vertically. The oblique line is the relationship between S and e^{min} derived in annex 1A: a *high* value of S maps into a *low* value of e^{min} because high sunk costs make exit followed by reentry a costly option, making the firm more tolerant of losses.

Figure 1.10   Sunk Costs and the Frequency of Exits

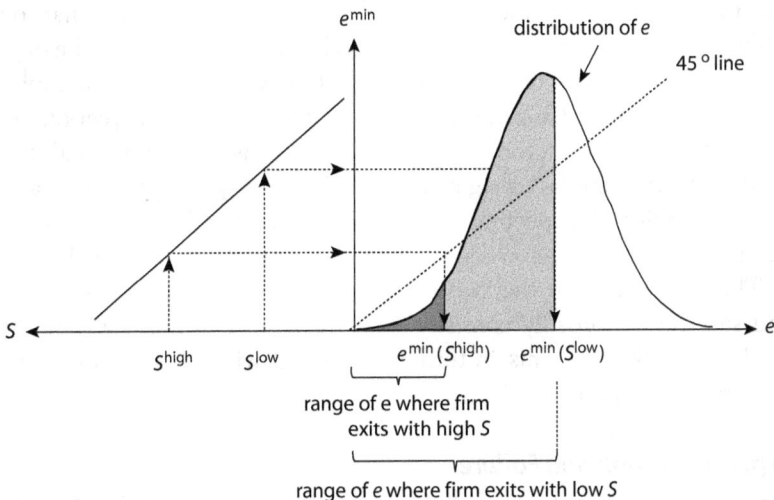

Consider now the right-hand side of the diagram. The exchange rate, e, is measured on the horizontal axis, increasing to the right. The bell-shaped curve is the distribution of the exchange rate, a random variable. Through the 45° line, a low value of e^{min} generates the small, dark range of exchange-rate draws for which the firm decides to exit the export market. A high value of e^{min} generates the larger, pale gray range of exchange-rate draws inducing exit.

Combining the two parts of the diagram, the high sunk cost S^{high} maps into a low e^{min}, which in turn generates a small exit range, whereas the low sunk cost S^{low} maps into a high value of e^{min} that generates a large exit range. Thus, the frequency of exit is higher with S^{low} than with S^{high}, which implies lower average survival with S^{low} than with S^{high}.

Working the relationship highlighted in figure 1.10 backward, the evidence of generally low survival reviewed earlier suggests that sunk costs of entry and exit must be low. Why should we worry about low survival, then? High turnover would be optimal in the presence of small sunk costs.

Existing empirical evidence on hysteresis at the firm level suggests that sunk costs of entry are indeed present, but that they may not be over-whelming. In a seminal paper that shifted the hysteresis literature's focus from aggregate flows to firms, Roberts and Tybout (1997) showed how expressing a plant's current export status as a function of the previous year's status made it possible to uncover evidence of sunk costs of entry. For instance, they found that a plant having exported in the previous year was up to 60 percent more likely to be currently exporting than one without previous-year export experience. However, they found the expe-rience effect to be short-lived, vanishing after two years without export-ing. They also found substantial turnover, with an average year-on-year exit rate of 11 percent. Similarly, Bernard and Jensen (2004) found, for a sample of U.S. manufacturing plants, that previous-year experience raised the probability of exporting by 39 percent, although they also found substantial turnover (an average annual exit rate of 12.6 percent).

The evidence from the two existing bodies of literature—sunk costs and survival—is broadly consistent and suggestive of nonnegligible but moderate sunk costs. This, in turn, is consistent with the recent evidence on export entrepreneurship.

Experimentation and Failure

Returning to our earlier analogy to population dynamics, in the presence of high infant mortality rates, overall mortality increases with birth rates because more births mean more infants who tend to die young. Do we observe high "birth rates" in terms of exports in low-income countries?

A number of papers—including, among others, Brenton, Pierola, and von Uexkull (2009) and Cadot, Carrère, and Strauss-Kahn (2011) (see also the survey in Brenton et al. 2009)—showed that export entrepreneurship at the "extensive margin," measured by the introduction of new products and new destinations, was very active in low-income countries. This is shown by the hump in figure 1.11, which occurs at less than US$10,000 PPP.

One would expect active export entrepreneurship to fuel overall export growth. However, Amurgo-Pacheco and Pierola (2007), Besedes and Prusa (2011), Brenton and Newfarmer (2007), and Evenett and Keller (2002) all found that the extensive margin's contribution to overall export growth was limited—although, interestingly, less so in Sub-Saharan Africa, where it accounts for over a third of export growth (figure 1.12). How can we explain this relatively small contribution, and does it relate to survival?

The smallness of the extensive margin's contribution—in spite of its strong activity—is due, in part, to the fact that many of the new products and destinations introduced in a given year will fail as early as the

Figure 1.11   Number of New Export Lines (HS 6) against Income Levels

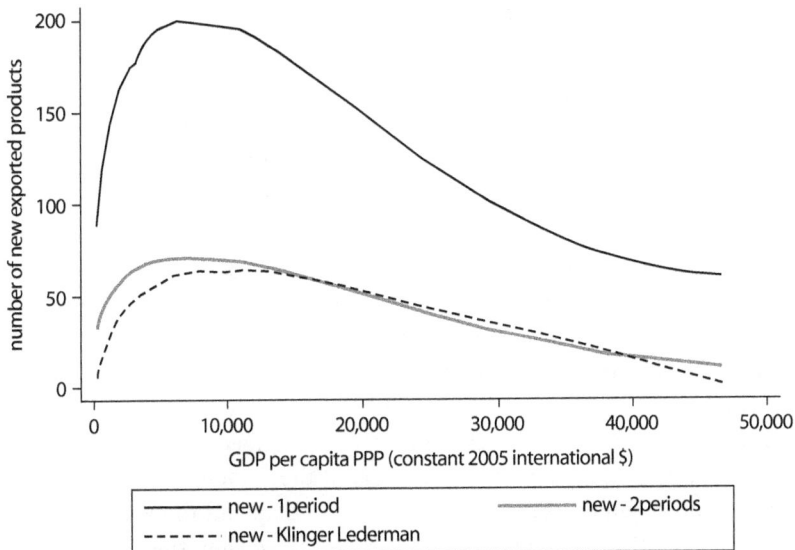

Source: Cadot, Carrère, and Strauss-Kahn 2011.

Figure 1.12   Export Growth Decomposed, 1990–2005

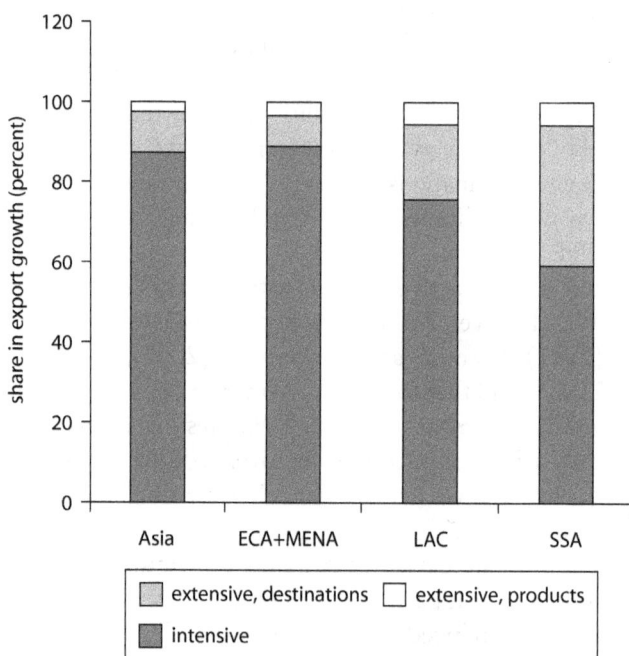

Source: Amurgo-Pacheco and Pierola 2007.
Note: ECA = Europe and Central Asia; MENA = the Middle East and North Africa; LAC = Latin America and the Caribbean; and SSA = Sub-Saharan Africa.

next. First-year survival rates are particularly low for low-income countries (39 percent, on average, as reported by Brenton, Saborowski, and von Uexkull 2010) and for Sub-Saharan Africa (33 percent). For Burkina Faso, the first-year survival rate is as low as 27 percent. Clearly, a lot of the experimentation fails.

The high infant mortality of African exports provides strong evidence of Darwinism—ensuring the survival of the fittest. It is also the reflection of a very tough environment, in which many export experiments fail for good or bad reasons. These reasons need to be understood in order to reduce the incidence of accidental deaths of viable export spells. This report will attempt to provide evidence in support of a number of conjectures, but before we turn to a systematic exploration of the evidence, we can use the simple setup of annex 1A in a first effort to understand the issue.

Export relationships can be terminated by either the exporter or the importer side, and importer decisions are likely to be driven by considerations distinct from those of exporters. Importers may, like exporters, have sunk costs in the relationship with individual suppliers, making switching to new suppliers costly. This will typically be the case in markets where search costs are high because of the presence of heterogeneity in quality and weak signaling (for example, through lack of enforceable warrantees) on the supplier side. Alternatively, importers may be able to switch easily from one supplier to another in deep, liquid markets with little product differentiation. This will typically be the case in markets, such as low-end garments, where search costs are low.

Annex 1A shows that a high probability of the termination of relationships by buyers has two effects on export survival. First, frequent terminations mechanically reduce the life expectancy of export spells. Second, and more interestingly, the expectation of frequent termination inhibits the willingness of exporters to tough it out in bad times, in the same way that it inhibits their willingness to invest in the relationship. This further reduces the life expectancy of export spells. By contrast, uncertainty in the sense of a high volatility of profits on the export market *raises* exporter willingness to stay in bad times because of an asymmetry in the effects of upside and downside risk, known in the real-options literature as the *good-news principle*. This principle says that only the upside potential matters for the willingness to keep a business line open, so more uncertainty makes the business line more persistent (see annex 1A for more details).

As a last conceptual observation, changes in the environment in which exporting firms operate can have complex effects on survival because they may trigger two types of reactions working at cross-purposes: (1) changes in the incentives faced by exporting firms and (2) changes in the composition of the population of exporting firms. To see this, suppose that the business environment becomes, in some sense, gentler—that is, more conducive to both entry and survival. In this case, on one hand each firm has a higher survival probability; on the other hand, exporting markets will attract inexperienced or low-productivity entrants that are more likely to fail. One might imagine a situation where the second effect dominates the first, so that an *improved* business environment *reduces* average survival rates.[8]

Preliminary evidence for this conjecture can be gathered by plotting average first-year survival rates of entering exporters (the probability of surviving past the first year of exports conditional on entry) against their average entry rates (the ratio of new entrants to the stock of exporters).

Controlling for other determinants of survival (reflecting business environment), the relationship is shown in figure 1.13.

On the sample shown in figure 1.13, there is indeed a negative correlation between entry rates and survival rates, suggesting a strong selection effect. It is possible that both variables react in the same way to changes in omitted variables; for instance, Araujo and Ornelas (2007) show in a theoretical model that improved contract enforcement raises both the entry and the persistence of existing trade relationships. However, the scatter plot of the figure is drawn from a regression where other covariates are included, limiting the scope—although not eliminating it—for omitted-variable bias.

Figure 1.13   Entry and First-Year Entrants' Survival Rates at the Firm Level

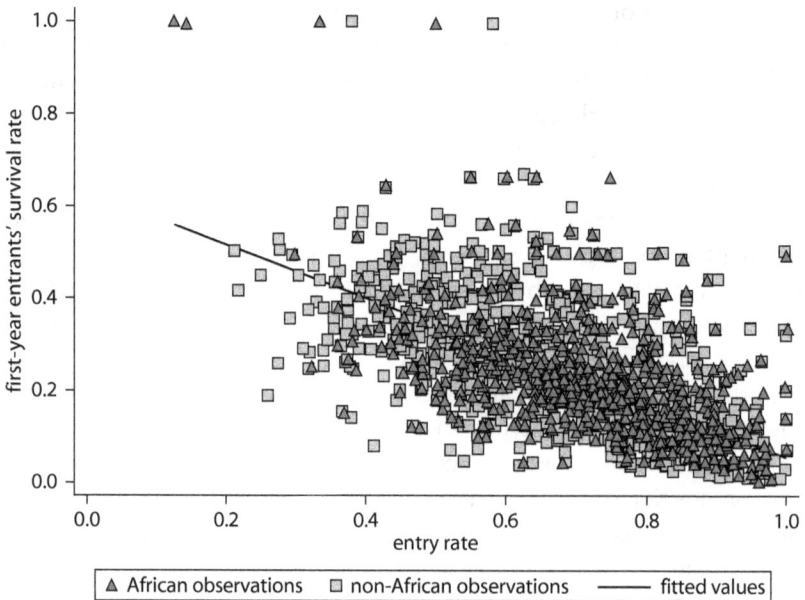

Source: Exporter Dynamics Database, Trade and International Integration Unit, Research Department, World Bank (DECTI). Available at: http://econ.worldbank.org/exporter-dynamics-database.
Note: Data points in this graph reflect average entry and survival rates for the period 2004–09 for each available HS 2-digit–country combination. The graph uses information from the Exporter Dynamics Database built by the Trade and International Integration Unit of the Research Department of the World Bank (DECTI). The entry and first-year survival rates used for this graph are for almost 30 developing countries in different regions around the world. The variable on the vertical axis is the first-year survival rate purged of the influence of other covariates (variables within the Trading Across Borders topic of Doing Business and variables other than the entry rate [horizontal axis]) using predicted coefficients from a linear probability model. Triangles indicate African observations.

This discussion can be summarized as follows:

- Sunk costs of entry and exit into export markets, such as search costs, raise export survival; the empirical evidence on the extent of such costs is so far limited and ambiguous.
- Fixed and variable costs of exporting (paperwork, representations abroad, and the array of trade-cost factors typically included in gravity equations) reduce export survival; the empirical evidence on the extent of such costs is substantial.
- Different types of uncertainty have sharply different effects on export survival:
  - a high volatility of prices and earnings on export markets raises survival, and
  - a high probability of buyer-determined termination reduces it.
- Survival rates may increase or decrease with entry rates when firms are heterogeneous in some unobserved ability to survive; thus, changes in the business environment (which also have an effect on average entry rates) have an ambiguous effect on average survival.

We will build on these very preliminary considerations in chapter 2 to explore systematically the drivers of export survival.

Annex 1A: The Basic Analytics of Survival

This annex uses a simple model of uncertainty with sunk cost to illustrate the determinants of a firm's decision to stay in the export business or to exit in the face of temporarily negative returns. The model is based on the real-options approach to decisions under uncertainty, laid out in Dixit (1989) and Dixit and Pyndyck (1994). A rigorous, infinite-horizon model can be found in Roberts and Tybout (1997); see also Clerides, Lach, and Tybout (1998) for a model with entry costs and learning.

Let p be the price of a widget the firm is exporting on a foreign market; $y(p,c)$, its profit-maximizing supply of widgets; F and c, the fixed and variable costs of production, respectively; and e, the exchange rate of the country in which the firm is selling. The exchange rate is expressed as the price of the foreign currency in home currency, so it goes up when the foreign currency appreciates.

Assume two periods, $t = 0$ and $t = 1$, with a discount factor $\delta = 1/(1 + r)$. At $t = 0$, the exchange rate is e_0. At $t = 1$, it is a random variable $\tilde{e}$ with the following distribution:

$$\Pr(\tilde{e} = e) = \begin{cases} q & \text{if } e = e^+, \\ 1 - q & \text{if } e = e^-. \end{cases} \quad (1)$$

At $t = 0$, the firm's profit function is

$$\pi_0 \equiv \pi(e_0) = (e_0 p - c) y(p,c) - F \quad (2)$$

and its expected profit at $t = 1$ is

$$\begin{aligned} E[\pi(\tilde{e})] &= q[(e^+ p - c) y(p,c) - F] + (1 - q)[(e^- p - c) y(p,c) - F] \\ &= (\bar{e} p - c) y(p,c) - F, \end{aligned} \quad (3)$$

where $\bar{e} = q e^+ + (1 - q) e^-$. Assume that

A1. $\pi_0 < 0$

A2. $\pi_0 + \delta \bar{\pi} < 0$ $\quad (4)$

A3. $\pi_0 + \delta q \pi^+ > 0$.

The first two inequalities imply that the firm is losing money at $t = 0$ given the exchange rate, and expected profit given the distribution of the exchange rate at $t = 1$ is also negative. Should the firm stay in that export market? Given A1 and A2, a simple Net Present Value (NPV) calculation suggests no. However, this answer, based on a simple NPV calculation, can be misleading in the presence of irreversibility or sunk costs or entry.

Consider first irreversibility. The firm has two options: (1) exiting now, with no possibility of reentry, or (2) waiting one period and then deciding, upon resolution of the exchange-rate uncertainty, to stay or to go. Under option 1, expected profit is

$$\pi_{out} = 0, \quad (5)$$

whereas under option 2, the firm incurs a loss $\pi_0 < 0$ in the current period but keeps the option of staying in the market at $t = 1$ upon good news, which will happen with probability q. If the news is bad, then it will exit. Thus, the value of staying is

$$\pi_{stay} = \pi_0 + \delta q \pi^+, \quad (6)$$

which is positive by A3. The difference between (6) and (5) is the value of the option to stay, which is here strictly positive. The firm should therefore stay in the face of current losses and even a negative expected payoff.

The stripped-down setup of equations (1) through (4) illustrates something known as the *good-news principle*—namely, a decision to quit a business line is linked only to its upside potential, not to its downside potential. To see this, observe that neither (5) nor (6) depends on π^-, the value of profits under a low realization of the exchange rate. The reason is that in that "state of nature," the firm will quit; so the decision depends only on π^+, the value of profits under a high realization of the exchange rate, in which the firm will stay. This principle has an important implication: more uncertainty, in the form of a mean-preserving spread in the distribution of profits on the export markets, *increases* hysteresis and therefore survival. This is highly counterintuitive: one would expect volatility of the destination-market environment to *reduce* survival, not to increase it. How can we make sense of this surprising implication of real-options theory? With more uncertainty, it is as if our exporting firm held an option on a more volatile stock—the upside potential, which is all that matters with a call option, is then higher, which makes the option more valuable.

Consider now another type of uncertainty—namely, the possibility that the buyer may terminate the relationship for reasons that are unknown to the exporter. Let Q be the probability that this happens at $t = 1$. Then (6) becomes

$$\pi_{\text{stay}} = \pi_0 + \delta q(1 - Q)\pi^+, \qquad (7)$$

which is decreasing in Q. If Q is sufficiently high, (7) becomes negative (under A1, it *must* turn negative when Q approaches 1), in which case the firm will never decide to stay in the export market, irrespective of q and π^+. This type of uncertainty, which is related to the buyer's behavior, has a completely different effect on hysteresis than a wider dispersion of second-period profits has. It depresses the firm's incentive to stay in the export market. The reason for this debilitating effect is that uncertainty in the form of a probability of an exogenous termination entails only downside risk and no upside risk, which means that the good-news principle does not apply.

This second result about the effect of uncertainty has very important implications for export survival. Erratic buyer practices—abrupt decisions to switch from one supplier to another in order to arbitrage very small price differences, which are common in sectors, such as garments, where price competition is intense—have a double effect on export survival, both direct and indirect. The direct effect is that each buyer-determined interruption reduces the life expectancy of export spells. The indirect effect, illustrated here, is that this lower life expectancy makes exporters less willing to endure hard times, because it cuts into the upside potential of the real option.

Suppose now that there is a sunk cost of reentry S. Expression (5) now becomes

$$\pi_{out} = \delta q(\pi^+ - S),\tag{8}$$

so the value of the option to stay is worth only

$$\Delta \pi = \pi_{stay} - \pi_{out} = \pi_0 - \delta q S.\tag{9}$$

We can now derive the lowest value of π_0 at which the firm is willing to stay on the market in the face of losses. The lower it is, the longer the export survival, our magnitude of interest. This value is such that

$$\pi_0 - \delta q S = 0$$

or, substituting for π_0 and rearranging,

$$(e_0 p - c) y(p,c) - F = -\delta q S,\tag{10}$$

which gives

$$e_0^{min} = \frac{1}{p}\left[c + \frac{F - \delta q S}{y(p,c)}\right].\tag{11}$$

It is easily verifiable that e_0^{min} is decreasing in the sunk cost, as

$$\frac{\partial e_0^{min}}{\partial S} = \frac{-\delta q}{py(p,c)} < 0.\tag{12}$$

That is, higher sunk costs of reentry encourage the firm to tough it out in the face of losses, because it makes exit and possible reentry tomorrow a costlier option. By contrast,

$$\frac{\partial e_0^{min}}{\partial F} = \frac{1}{py(p,c)} > 0.\tag{13}$$

That is, higher fixed costs make staying a more expensive option—recall that the options we are considering are staying and exiting, not shutting down while still incurring fixed costs, which is an entirely different decision. Thus, higher fixed costs reduce the patience of the firm with low realizations of the exchange rate (the unique source of uncertainty in our model). Similarly, it is easily verified that

$$\frac{\partial e_0^{min}}{\partial c} = \frac{1}{p} - \frac{\delta q S}{p y^2} \frac{\partial y}{\partial c} > 0. \tag{14}$$

This tension between fixed (or variable) and sunk costs is at the heart of the analysis of hysteresis (see Baldwin and Krugman 1989 for further elaboration). The negative effect of fixed costs on the willingness to stay in export markets during bad times justifies the use of gravity-type variables as determinants of average export-spell duration. The positive effect of sunk costs is explored through indirect proxies in chapter 2.

Annex 1B: The Basic Toolkit of Empirical Survival Analysis

This annex introduces the basic techniques of applied survival analysis. A good introduction is provided by Volpe and Carballo (2009). For a complete, hands-on introduction to survival analysis, see Cleves et al. (2010). Two key characteristics of survival data sets must be kept in mind to understand the analysis' specificities.

First, time is defined as "analytical time" rather than calendar or clock time. Analytical time is individual-specific and is set at zero when an individual starts being "at risk." For instance, the zero of analytical time may be when an individual enters a treatment, a light bulb is put under a test, or an export spell begins.

Second, observations are "spells" from the zero of analytical time to the individual's death (for example, the failure of the light bulb or the termination of the export relationship). Outside of laboratory experiments, because the sample period is not infinite, some spells will be "left-censored" (that is, they will already be active when the sample period starts) or "right-censored" (that is, they will not be completed when the sample period ends). Left-censored spells are typically dropped out of the sample, whereas right-censored ones are treated explicitly by the econometric procedures of survival analysis. When dealing with trade data, many countries fail to report trade flows in some years, creating right- and left-censoring in the middle of the sample period that must be treated carefully. This can be checked using the data-availability file in the "support-material" menu of the World Integrated Trade Solution portal. Holes in the data can be partially filled by using mirroring (which should be done systematically for the entire data set).

Kaplan-Meier Survival Functions

The Kaplan-Meier nonparametric estimator, sometimes called the *product-limit estimator,* approximates the survivor function defined as follows. Let T be the duration of a given export spell (a random variable) and t be a particular, arbitrary value of T. The survivor function is the probability that failure takes place at or after t—that is, that survival is at least T:

$$S(t) = \Pr(T \geq t) = 1 - F(t), \tag{1}$$

where *F(t)* is the cumulative distribution function of the failure time.

Consider now several spells, and let i be an index of time going from the beginning of spells to their death. That is, suppose we observe a sample of N spells whose duration varies between one and ten years. Then $i = 1, \ldots, 10$. Let k_i be the number of spells that die exactly at i years, and n_i be the number of spells that are still alive after i years. The Kaplan-Meier estimate of $S(t)$ is

$$\hat{S}(t) = \prod_{i=1}^{t} \left(1 - \frac{k_i}{n_i} \right). \tag{2}$$

The ratio in the parentheses is the ratio of spells dying to spells at risk; thus, it is the discrete-time equivalent of a hazard rate. The Kaplan-Meier estimate of the survivor function in the first year is the proportion of spells that do not die in the first year. Its estimate in the second year is the product of that by the proportion of spells that do not die in the second year (among those still alive); and so on. Obviously, since each term is less than one, it is a decreasing function (see figures 1.6 and 1.7 for examples).

Differences in survival pattern between two groups can be tested using, for instance, a log-rank test, which is a comparison of distributions adapted to a setting where some observations are censored (see above). The test statistic follows a chi-square with two degrees of freedom for a pairwise comparison.

Cox Regressions

Cox regressions explain hazard rates (death/termination probabilities) in terms of individual covariates, under particular assumptions. The hazard rate of a distribution is the probability that an event (here, death) occurs in the next instant, given that it has not happened yet. Formally,

$$h(t) = \lim_{\Delta t \to 0} \Pr\left(T \le t + \Delta t \,\middle|\, T \ge t\right)$$
$$= \frac{f(t)}{1 - F(t)} = \frac{f(t)}{S(t)}.$$

(3)

In the discrete-time framework that is relevant for empirical analysis,

$$h(t) = \Pr\ (T = t \,|\, T \ge t),\ t = 1, 2, \ldots$$

The fundamental assumption of Cox regression, called *proportional hazards*, is that individual hazard rates can be decomposed into two multiplicative components:

o   a component that varies with analytical time but is common to all individuals, $h_0(t)$; and

o   a component that varies across individuals, as an (exponential) function of a vector of covariates, but not over time, $\exp(\mathbf{x}\boldsymbol{\beta})$.

That is,

$$h(t) = h_0(t)e^{\mathbf{x}\boldsymbol{\beta}}.$$

(4)

A Cox regression is estimated by maximum likelihood. Parameter estimates for the β's give partial correlations between each of the covariates and the hazard rate; thus, a positive coefficient indicates that a particular covariate *raises* the probability of termination and therefore contributes negatively to survival. Coefficients can also be reported as hazard ratios—that is, exponentiated coefficients; an exponentiated coefficient above one indicates that a covariate raises the hazard rate. To see the logic of this, consider a "dummy" covariate that can be either zero or one and call it I :

$$E(h \,|\, I = 1) = h_0(t)e^{\beta},$$

(5)

whereas

$$E(h \,|\, I = 0) = h_0(t)e^0 = h_0(t).$$

(6)

Thus, the ratio of the hazard rates when $I = 1$ vs. when $I = 0$ is $h_0(t)e^{\beta} / h_0(t) = e^{\beta}$. If $e^{\beta} > 1$, then $\beta > 0$. The Cox functional form, in which hazard rates vary across individuals independently of time (the proportional-hazards assumption), can be verified by a Schönfeld test.

Notes

1. Throughout, we use the SITC nomenclature rather than the newer and more detailed Harmonized System (HS). This is because the SITC has undergone fewer revisions over time and offers longer time series, which is preferable for survival analysis. Our sample period will typically be 1979–2010.

2. The trade data tell us when firms commence, continue, and stop exporting a particular product to a specific market. They do not tell us how many firms enter or when particular firms exit.

3. Typically, customs monitors imports better than exports because tariffs are levied on the former. Accordingly, the survival of export flows is measured using import-side trade statistics rather than export-side ones, a technique known as *mirroring*. For instance, we would measure the survival of our Pakistan-Japan trade flow using Japan's import statistics rather than Pakistan's export statistics. Still, inputting errors in automated customs recording systems such as Automated System for Customs Data/Système Douanier Automatisé (ASYCUDA/SYDONIA) or others are frequent, in particular when entries are made directly by customs brokers.

4. Their baseline results are obtained on more disaggregated data (22,782 observations over 1989–2001) but we will stick to SITC-4 data, which will be used throughout this report because it is the finest level at which data are comparable across countries.

5. Besedes and Prusa (2006b) applied the weighting scheme on SITC-5 data, for which the unweighted average duration was 4.1 years.

6. High-income non-OECD countries include Croatia, Cyprus, Hong Kong SAR, China, Kuwait, Saudi Arabia, Singapore, and the United Arab Emirates (UAE). They are mostly small countries, many of which are platforms for entrepôt trade (for example, the UAE or Singapore).

7. *Mirroring* consists of using import flows as reported by the importing country instead of export flows, which are monitored less accurately since customs authorities generally give greater attention to products entering their customs space and eligible for domestic duties.

8. We are grateful to Caroline Freund for attracting our attention to this point.

References

Acharya, Rohini, J. A. Crawford, M. Mariszewska, and C. Renard. 2011. "Landscape." In *Preferential Trade Agreement Policies for Development: A Handbook*, ed. J.-P. Chauffour and J.-C. Maur, 37–67. Washington, DC: World Bank.

Amurgo-Pacheco, Alberto, and M. D. Pierola. 2007. "Patterns of Export Diversification in Developing Countries: Intensive and Extensive Margins." Policy Research Working Paper 4473, World Bank, Washington, DC.

Araujo, Luis, and E. Ornelas. 2007. "Trust-Based Trade." CEP Discussion Paper 0820. Centre for Economic Performance, London.

Baldwin, Richard. 1988. "Hysteresis in Import Prices: The Beachhead Effect." *American Economic Review* 78: 773–85.

Baldwin, Richard, and P. Krugman. 1989. "Persistent Effects of Large Exchange-Rate Shocks." *Quarterly Journal of Economics* 104: 635–54.

Bernard, Andrew B., and J. B. Jensen. 2004. "Why Some Firms Export." *Review of Economics and Statistics* 86: 561–69.

Besedes, Tibor, and J. Blyde. 2010. "What Drives Export Survival? An Analysis of Export Duration in Latin America." Draft, Inter-American Development Bank.

Besedes, Tibor, and T. Prusa. 2006a. "Product Differentiation and Duration of U.S. Import Trade." *Journal of International Economics* 104: 635–54.

———. 2006b. "Ins, Outs, and the Duration of Trade." *Canadian Journal of Economics* 39: 266–95.

———. 2011. "The Role of the Extensive and Intensive Margins and Export Growth." *Journal of Development Economics* 96 (2): 371–79.

Brenton, Paul, and R. Newfarmer. 2007. "Watching More than the Discovery Channel: Export Cycles and Diversification in Development." Policy Research Working Paper 4302, World Bank, Washington, DC.

Brenton, Paul, R. Newfarmer, W. Shaw, and P. Walkenhorst. 2009. "Breaking into New Markets: Overview." In *Breaking into New Markets: Emerging Lessons for Export Diversification*, ed. R. Newfarmer, W. Shaw, and P. Walkenhorst, 1–38. Washington, DC: World Bank.

Brenton, Paul, M. D. Pierola, and J. E. von Uexkull. 2009. "The Life and Death of Trade Flows: Understanding the Survival Rates of Developing-Country Exporters." In *Breaking into New Markets: Emerging Lessons for Export Diversification*, ed. R. Newfarmer, W. Shaw, and P. Walkenhorst, 127–44. Washington, DC: World Bank.

Brenton, Paul, C. Saborowski, and J. E. von Uexkull. 2010. "What Explains the Low Survival Rate of Developing Country Export Flows?" *World Bank Economic Review* 24 (3): 474–99.

Cadot, Olivier, C. Carrère, and V. Strauss-Kahn. 2011. "Export Diversification: What's Behind the Hump?" *Review of Economics & Statistics* 93: 590–605.

Carrère, Céline, and V. Strauss-Kahn. 2011. "Exports that Last: When Experience Matters." Draft, University of Geneva.

Clerides, Sofronis, S. Lach, and J. Tybout. 1998. "Is Learning by Exporting Import? Micro-Dynamic Evidence from Colombia." *Quarterly Journal of Economics* 113: 903–47.

Cleves, Mario, W. Gould, R. Gutierrez, and Y. Marchenko. 2010. *An Introduction to Survival Analysis Using Stata*, 3rd ed. College Station, TX: Stata Press.

Dixit, Avinash. 1989. "Entry and Exit Decisions under Uncertainty." *Journal of Political Economy* 97 (2): 620–38.

Dixit, Avinash, and R. Pindyck. 1994. *Investment under Uncertainty*. Princeton, NJ: Princeton University Press.

Easterly, William, and A. Resheff. 2010. "African Export Successes: Surprises, Stylized Facts, and Explanations." NBER Working Paper 16597, National Bureau of Economic Research, Cambridge, MA.

Evenett, Simon J., and W. Keller. 2002. "On Theories Explaining the Success of the Gravity Equation." *Journal of Political Economy* 110 (2): 281–316.

Evenett, Simon, and A. Venables. 2002. "Export Growth by Developing Economies: Market Entry and Bilateral Trade." Draft, University of St. Gallen.

Fugazza, Marco, and A. C. Molina. 2011. "On the Determinants of Exports Survival." Policy Issues in International Trade and Commodities Study Series No. 46. UNCTAD, New York and Geneva.

Krugman, Paul. 1986. "Pricing to Market When the Exchange Rate Changes." NBER Working Paper 1926, National Bureau of Economic Research, Cambridge, MA.

Nitsch, Volker. 2009. "Die Another Day: Duration in German Import Trade." *Weltwirtschaftliches Archiv* 145: 133–54.

Roberts, Mark, and J. Tybout. 1997. "The Decision to Export in Colombia: An Empirical Model of Entry with Sunk Costs." *American Economic Review* 87: 545–64.

Volpe, Christian, and J. Carballo. 2009. "Survival of New Exporters in Developing Countries: Does It Matter How They Diversify?" Inter-American Development Bank Working Paper IDB-WP-140, IADB, Washington, DC.

World Bank. *World Development Indicators*. Available at: http://data.worldbank .org/data-catalog/world-development-indicators.

CHAPTER 2

Countries, Institutions, and Policies

In this chapter, we turn to some of the most policy-relevant determinants of export survival at the country level—including supply-side factors such as comparative advantage and the business environment as well as demand-side ones—with a focus on standards and technical regulations, and on the way they are enforced in industrial countries.

In traditional Heckscher-Ohlin trade theory, comparative advantage conditions the viability of exports and therefore their sustainability. Whereas the relationship of comparative advantage to the direction and magnitude of trade flows has been subjected to many tests, starting with the celebrated Leontieff paradox, its relationship to export sustainability has not. Yet this latter relationship is important for policy design. Many recent papers (see, for instance, Dutt, Mihov, and van Zandt 2008 and Hausmann, Hwang, and Rodrik 2007) suggest that the composition of a country's export basket matters for its future growth. These findings may be interpreted as meaning that active export-promotion policies should be used to upgrade the positioning of a country's export portfolio. However, we find that products lying far from a country's comparative advantage stand less chance of surviving on world markets. Thus, policies promoting those products may produce false starts and prove costly.

Beyond traditional factors of production—labor, physical capital, human capital, and natural resources—export performance is largely conditioned by the business environment in the exporting country. We show, on the basis of a novel data set, that this broad observation carries over to export survival, which correlates with various measures of trade costs and the business environment. In particular, we find that Sub-Saharan countries in the sample distinguish themselves not so much by their poor survival performance, but by their poor ratings in terms of the business environment, suggesting that this environment is a key constraint to export survival. The results of the statistical analysis align well with results of a survey of African exporters conducted by the World Bank as background to this report.

Finally, we highlight the potential role of standards in destination countries and their enforcement in the context of agricultural exports to Western countries. We argue through anecdotal evidence that enforcement may be discretionary and may lead to an abrupt interruption of supply chains, potentially creating the debilitating kind of uncertainty that was shown in annex 1A of chapter 1 to discourage exporters. We also suggest a perverse mechanism whereby intermediaries ensure their own survival essentially by shifting all the risk upstream to farmers.

In the first section of this chapter, we look for new evidence about the relationship between comparative advantage and the sustainability of exports. In the second section, we explore ways that the business environment in the origin and destination markets shapes the ability of firms to survive in export markets. And in the third section, we consider the effect that technical regulations and the enforcement of sanitary and phytosanitary standards has on destination markets.

Comparative Advantage

Export products located closer to a country's comparative advantage tend to survive, on average, better than those located farther away. *Comparative advantage* is the adequacy of a country's endowment of factors of production (labor, capital, human capital, and natural resources) to what is needed for the production of a particular export good. For instance, if a good is capital-intensive (e.g., the making of silicon wafers for microchips), a country has a comparative advantage in the production and export of that good if the country is capital-abundant. This relationship between factor intensity and factor abundance is, in essence, an expression of the Heckscher-Ohlin theorem. Comparative advantage translates into *competitive* advantage for firms exporting the good in question, provided that three basic conditions are fulfilled. First, macroeconomic fundamentals—in particular the exchange rate—must be "right"—that is, the exchange rate must not be overvalued. If the exchange rate is overvalued, even the production of silicon wafers in a capital-abundant country can fail to generate profits. Second, the basic infrastructure (e.g., roads and telecommunications) must be adequate. Producing shirts in a labor-abundant country can fail to generate profits if ports are dysfunctional or roadblocks are prevalent. Third, the investment climate (ease of doing business) must also be adequate. Meeting these conditions—comparative advantage, sound macroeconomic fundamentals, adequate infrastructure, and favorable investment climate—ensures, in a very broad sense, the sustainability of exports.

In a perfect world, firms would not enter export markets when the country where they are located has no comparative advantage, so one would expect comparative advantage to affect the *extensive margin* of trade—the probability of observing export flows—but not necessarily their *survival*. However, in reality, as we saw earlier in this report, there is a lot of experimentation. Firms try, fail, and try again. In the presence of intense experimentation, one might observe more success and therefore longer survival for goods exported in accordance with the origin country's pattern of comparative advantage.

Verifying this conjecture has been difficult, since neither endowments nor the factor intensities of goods were readily available in public databases. Recently, however, the United Nations Conference on Trade and Development (UNCTAD) has made public a new database that includes both endowments and factor intensities.[1] Endowments include the dollar value of physical capital per worker calculated from investment data using the perpetual inventory method, educational attainments (average years of education per worker), the labor force, arable land per worker, and the dollar value of subsoil (oil and mining) resources—although this last component of endowments, calculated by the World Bank, is available only for two years, 1994 and 2000.

Factor intensities are calculated as follows. The logic is that of Hausmann, Hwang, and Rodrik's (2007) PRODY. That is, the revealed capital intensity of product k is a weighted average of the capital endowments of all the countries exporting product k, the weights being modified versions of Balassa's revealed-comparative advantage index. Formally,

$$\hat{\kappa}_k = \sum_i \omega_{ik} \kappa_i, \qquad (1)$$

where κ_i is country i's capital/labor endowment and ω_{ik} is the modified Balassa index for country i and product k. The reason for not using simple export shares is that these would give too much weight to large countries, and the reason for modifying Balassa indexes is to make them add up to a total of 1, so that endowments and intensities can be shown in the same space (that is, in the same diagram). Human-capital intensities (that is, h_i for country i) are calculated in a way similar to (1).

We can now define comparative *disadvantage* (the opposite of comparative advantage) as the Euclidian distance between a country's endowment point (κ_i, h_i) and the intensity of product k$(\hat{\kappa}_k, \hat{h}_k)$:

$$d_{ik}^e = \left[\left(h_i - \hat{h}_k \right)^2 + \left(\kappa_i - \hat{\kappa}_k \right)^2 \right]^{1/2}. \tag{2}$$

Using that measure of product distance from the exporter's endowment point and our proxy for comparative disadvantage, figure 2.1 shows that average export spell survival decreases with comparative disadvantage, although the effect is limited (the vertical axis measures

Figure 2.1   Average Spell Survival and Comparative Disadvantage

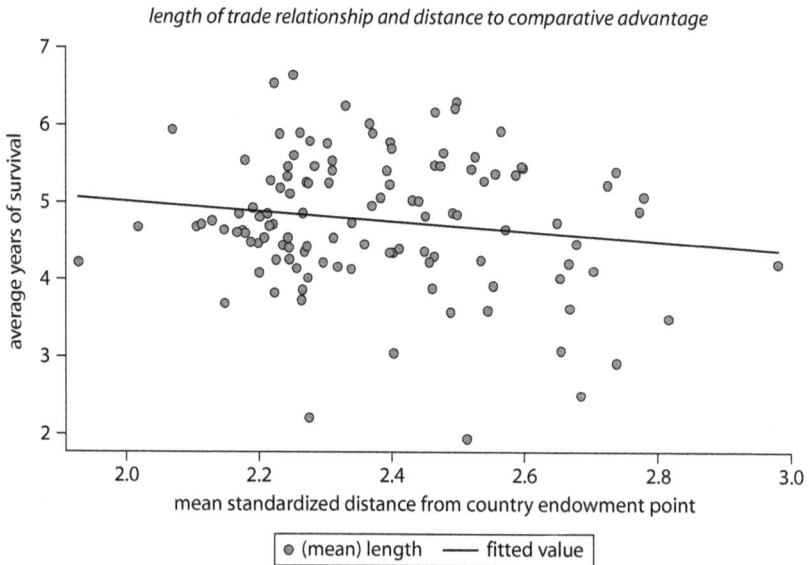

length of trade relationship and distance to comparative advantage

y-axis: average years of survival

x-axis: mean standardized distance from country endowment point

Legend: ● (mean) length   ——— fitted value

Source: Authors' calculations based on UN Comtrade database.
Note: Each point corresponds to an International Standard Industrial Classification (ISIC) Rev.3 industry average (117 manufacturing industries), aggregated over products and countries.

average years of survival, which means that going from the left-hand tail of the distribution of distances to its right-hand tail reduces average survival only from five to four years).[2] Stating the same assertion upside down, the probability of survival rises with comparative advantage.[3]

This result is important for its policy implications. Export-promotion agencies providing assistance to new exporters or to exporters wishing to expand their portfolio of offerings often perform some sort of informal screening of proposals based on the success and survival prospects of those offerings. This screening is often based on the officers' experience and the past record of the applying firm, at least for programs that have been running long enough to have a history. The results in this section suggest that some comparative-advantage criteria may help to formalize the screening process in order to improve the survival of promoted exports.

The discussion of comparative advantage so far has been static. Yet comparative advantage shifts over time as countries accumulate factors of production. Another way in which comparative advantage can impinge on survival is if countries travel relatively rapidly through "diversification cones," a process that makes the optimal export portfolio evolve rapidly from a comparative-advantage point of view. This is the gist of an argument laid out in Schott (2003) and illustrated in figure 2.2.

In the upper panel of figure 2.2, the horizontal axis measures the country's capital endowment whereas the vertical axis measures its constant labor endowment (the figure omits human capital for simplicity). In the bottom panel, the horizontal axis measures per capita income (which is assumed to be proportional to its capital endowment for a fixed labor force), and the vertical axis measures sectoral shares in exports. First, the country exploits its advantage in unskilled labor and increases its exports of products such as textiles and clothing. As the exporting country accumulates capital, it then leaves the most labor-intensive diversification cone and its attendant textile and apparel sector, which separates the first cone from the second. As textiles and apparels shrink, automobiles—which are more capital-intensive and separate the second cone from the third—expand and then shrink as additional capital is accumulated. As automobiles shrink in turn, chemicals—which are still more capital-intensive and separate the third cone from the fourth—also expand; with no other diversification cone, the chemicals sector does not decline.

Empirical evidence from a large panel of countries, shown in figure 2.3, supports this conjecture. In panel a, the share of exports of textiles and apparel in total exports grows very rapidly from the lowest

Figure 2.2   Traveling through Diversification Cones

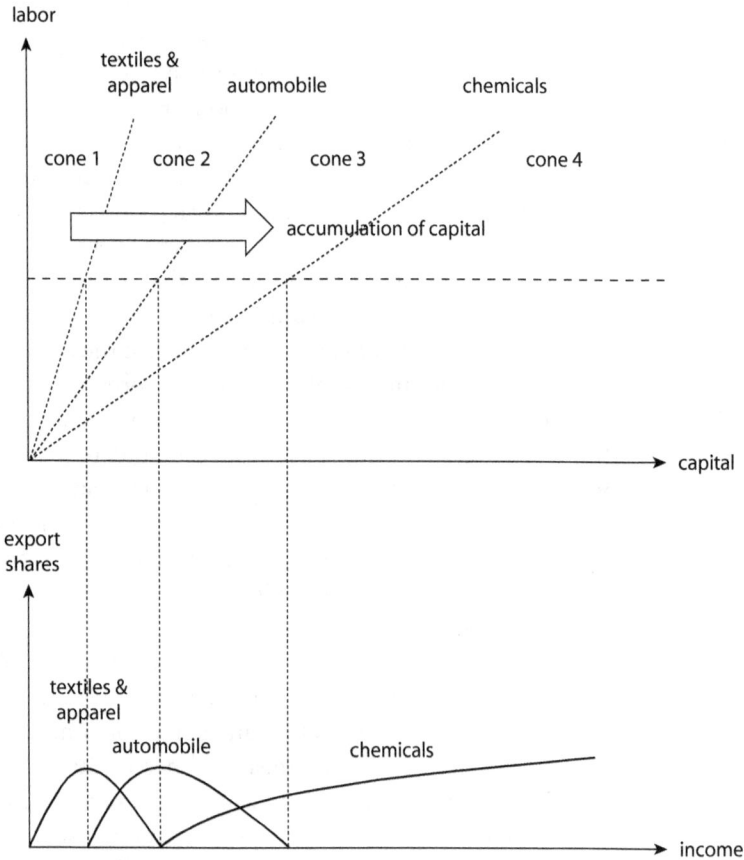

Source: Adapted from Schott 2003.

level of income and then declines continuously. In panel b, the share of transport equipment rises up to about $26,000 Purchasing Power Parity (PPP), then declines. In panel c, machinery rises to $30,000 PPP, then stays constant. Finally, in panel d, the export share of chemicals rises monotonically as a function of GDP per capita of countries.

Thus, a country's accumulation of capital generates a product cycle that is responsible for some of the observed births and deaths in export markets. That product cycle is likely to be long and is therefore unlikely to explain the short-run churning observed in the data. However, as some countries travel quickly across cones through rapid

Figure 2.3   Evolution of Sectoral Shares with Income Levels

a. textiles & apparel (section 11)

lowess smoother

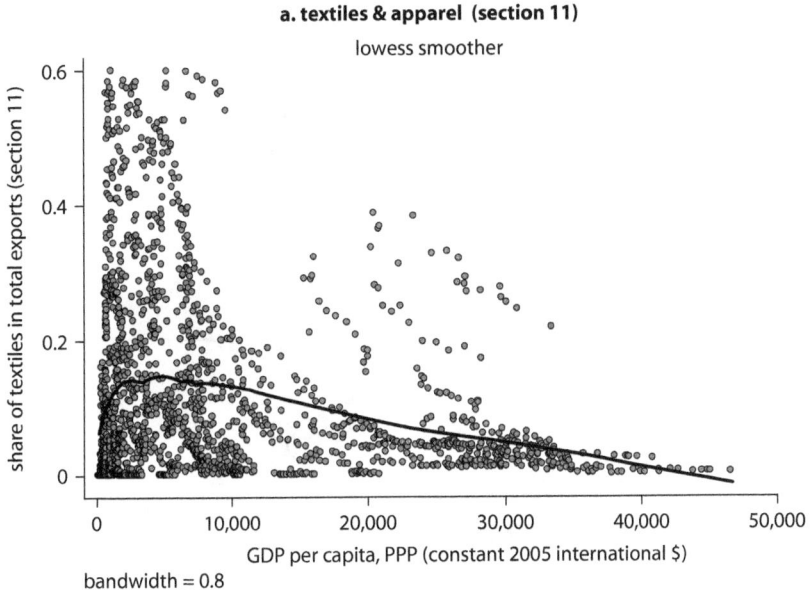

bandwidth = 0.8

b. transport equipment (section 17)

lowess smoother

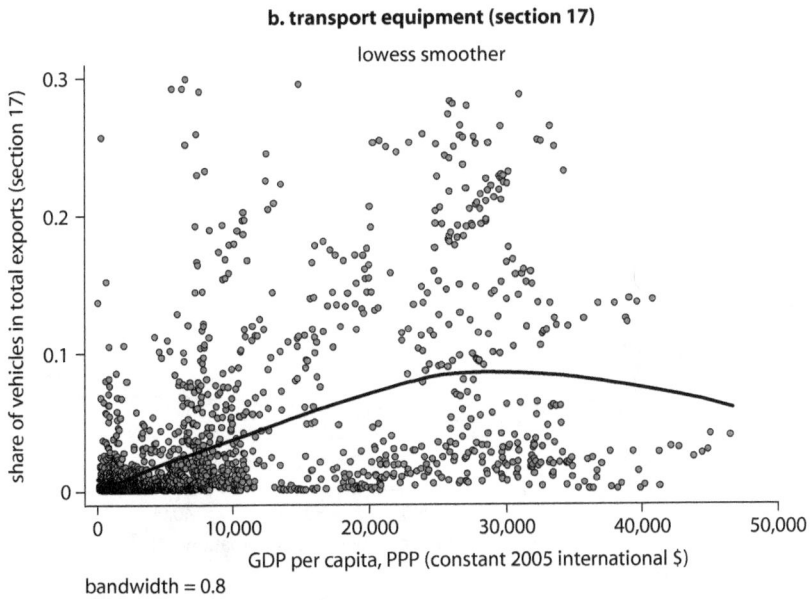

bandwidth = 0.8

(continued next page)

Figure 2.3   *(continued)*

c. machinery (section 16)

lowess smoother

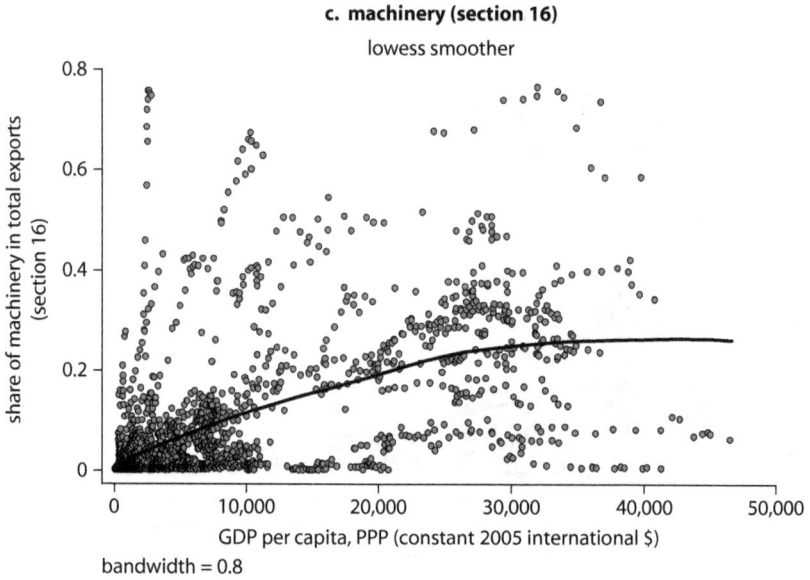

bandwidth = 0.8

d. chemicals (section 6)

lowess smoother

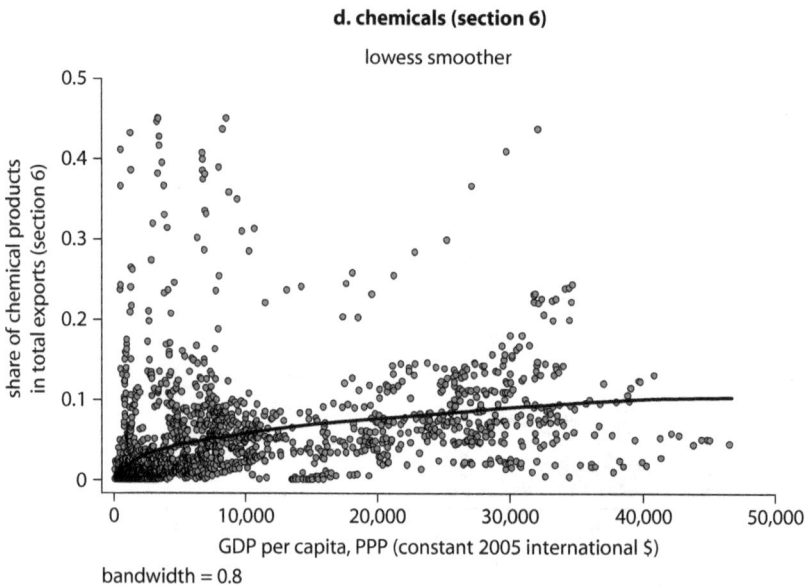

bandwidth = 0.8

Source: Cadot, Carrère, and Strauss-Kahn 2011.
Note: PPP = purchasing power parity

development, one should expect to observe an accelerated product cycle with exporters trying to go "one bridge too far"—either exporting products that will lie in the country's diversification cone, but too early, or exporting products in which the country is rapidly losing its comparative advantage, but too late. Thus, deaths at both tails of the distribution of factor intensities are likely to be more frequent when rapid change in the country's comparative advantage creates a rapidly evolving environment.

So far, the discussion of shifting comparative advantage has been cast in traditional Heckscher-Ohlin terms—that is, in terms of largely homogeneous products. In reality, most manufactured products are differentiated by their quality. As a country accumulates capital, technology, and know-how, it moves up the quality ladder within goods as well as across goods. In much the same way as traveling across diversification cones generates challenges that firms must meet to adapt to new circumstances, climbing up the quality ladder—often because lower-wage exporters are breathing down the neck of more traditional ones—creates adaptation challenges that firms must meet to survive.

In a rapidly shifting environment, export sustainability depends largely on the capacity of individual firms to adapt. Useful lessons on what drives firm resilience to shocks can be drawn from a case study of India's knitwear industry, which underwent a severe crisis in the early 1990s as a result of the loss of guaranteed markets in the Soviet Union and of India's trade liberalization. Tewari (1999) shows that the industry recovered very rapidly, shifting product mixes to suit the more demanding Western markets and getting back onto a strong growth trajectory. She provides an interesting account of the factors that contributed to the industry's resilience. Exporters that withstood the shock better than average included those with a strong position in the domestic market as well. In Tewari's words:

> The striking point in this regard is that these learning effects occurred in a segment of the domestic market that was dynamic despite being sheltered behind high tariff walls in a country that has long been maligned as an excessively dirigiste regime that has shackled productivity through its "disastrous" policies of import substitution (Tewari 1999, p. 1661).

Second, the more robust exporters included firms that adapted not only their investment policies, but also—and perhaps more important—their managerial practices. Third, she highlights the importance of a strong fabric of midsize companies:

> Middle-level firms with up to 300 to 500 workers, who have accumulated capital and have the resources to invest in new processes, have been able to take the fullest advantage of the opportunities created by the crisis of 1991 to restructure themselves quite radically. In contrast to the largest firms, this middle tier is more closely tied to the vast network of small firms and suppliers, and influences them in incremental ways—by forcing organizational changes among their suppliers, creating demand, and by "vacating" some segments of the export market where smaller firms are now able to compete (Tewari 1999, p. 1656).

Thus, industry structure interacts with individual firm capabilities to generate a sustainable and resilient export basis. It is therefore critical for the business environment in the exporting country to be conducive to the blossoming of this critical layer of midsize firms. In the Sub-Saharan African context, corruption, which is mentioned by many exporters as a key constraint (see below), is likely to be a particular hurdle precisely for those midsize firms that are too big to hide in the informal market and too small to have political connections.

Trade Costs and the Business Environment

The institutional environment in which business transactions take place—the term *transactions* taken in a broad sense to mean all the conditions and events surrounding a firm's activity, including, for example, customs and trade facilitation, contract enforcement, access to credit, and the tax and procedural environment—has also been shown in the recent literature to be a key determinant of trade flows. For instance, Levchenko (2007) and Nunn (2007) showed how institutional quality and contract enforcement could create endogenous comparative advantage.

In the case of Africa, while the predominance of primary-product exports is consistent with natural resource–based comparative advantage, the small share of exports of labor-intensive manufactured goods and the lack of transition to labor-intensive diversification cones reflect the poor infrastructure and weak regulatory environment that characterizes the continent and lead to very high trade costs. According to the ranking of 183 countries by the World Bank's Ease of Doing Business (2011), only 3 out of 46 African countries are within the top 50 countries (Mauritius in the 21st position, followed by South Africa in the 36th position, and Rwanda in the 50th); 30 are in the bottom 50, and almost all of the last 10 slots are all occupied by African nations. Overall, most of the African nations show a less-favorable business environment than countries in other regions.

Trade costs weigh heavily on the overall export performance of Sub-Saharan Africa, especially for cross-border trade within Africa. World Bank (2011) compares the prices of agricultural products in a wide range of markets in Burundi, the Democratic Republic of Congo, and Rwanda. The report concludes that the effect on relative prices of crossing the Burundi-Rwanda border is equivalent, on average, to pushing the two markets an additional 174 kilometers or 4.6 hours farther apart. However, crossing the Burundi–Democratic Republic of Congo border is equivalent, on average, to pushing markets in each country 1,824 kilometers or 41 hours farther apart, and crossing the Democratic Republic of Congo–Rwanda border is equivalent to adding an extra 1,549 kilometers and an additional 35 hours. This reflects the very high financial and physical costs associated with crossing the Democratic Republic of Congo border.

Non-tariff barriers to trade are pervasive throughout Africa. Box 2.1 provides examples from southern Africa and indicates the costs that are

---

Box 2.1

Examples of Non-Tariff Barriers and Their Costs in Southern Africa

Inefficiencies in transport, customs, and logistics raise trade costs: For regional trade agreements to be effective, it is critical that intraregional trade be able to move without hindrance. However, high transaction costs are being incurred because of inadequate transport infrastructure and inefficiencies in customs procedures (including delays at road checks, borders, and ports) as well as poor quality and costly logistics that are the result of weak competition among service providers. For example, the supermarket chain Shoprite reports that each day that one of its trucks is delayed at a border costs the company US$500.

Restrictive rules of origin limit preferential trade: Onerous local content requirements in rules of origin (ROOs), particularly in labor-intensive sectors (such as clothing) that use capital-intensive inputs not produced competitively in the region (such as fabrics), reduce the incentive to trade regionally. For example, the

(continued next page)

Box 2.1 *(continued)*

implementation of more restrictive rules (double transformation) on selected clothing imports from Malawi, Mozambique, Tanzania, and Zambia resulted in some clothing producers in these countries (for example, Bidserv in Malawi) losing their ability to compete in the regional market. For other products where ROOs have been so contentious (such as wheat flour) or simply not agreed (for example, certain electrical products for which rules were finalized only in April 2010), preferential trade within the region has been effectively prohibited (Naumann 2008).

Further costs arise from the administrative requirements for certificates of origin, which can account for nearly half the value of the duty preference. For example, Shoprite spends US$5.8 million per year in dealing with red tape (for example, in filing certificates and obtaining import permits) to secure US$13.6 million in duty savings under the Southern African Development Community (SADC). Woolworths does not use SADC preferences at all in sending regionally produced consignments of food and clothing to its franchise stores in non–Southern African Customs Union (SACU) SADC markets. Instead, it simply pays full tariffs because it currently deems the process of administering the ROO documentation to be too costly.

Poorly designed technical regulations and standards limit consumer choice and hamper trade: Standards regimes in southern Africa are often characterized by an over-reliance on mandatory inspections and certifications; unique national (rather than regional or international) standards and testing; overlapping responsibilities for regulation; and, occasionally, heavy government involvement in all dimensions of the standards system. These factors create unnecessary barriers to trade, especially when technical regulations and standards are applied in a discriminatory fashion against imports. One example is shoes in Mauritius, where the Chamber of Commerce has proposed the development of a regulation to govern the quality of shoes to prevent the entry of low-cost Chinese sandals that are perceived to have a tendency to wear more quickly than domestically produced ones. However, these lower-quality shoes are often the only ones that the poorest people in Mauritius can afford to buy.

Other non-tariff barriers restrict opportunities for regional sourcing: Other barriers—such as trade permits, export taxes, import licenses, and bans—also persist. Shoprite, for example, spends US$20,000 per week on securing import

(continued next page)

Box 2.1 *(continued)*

permits to distribute meat, milk, and plant-based goods to its stores in Zambia alone. For all the countries in which it operates, approximately 100 (single-entry) import permits are applied for every week; this can rise to 300 per week in peak periods. As a result of these and other documentary requirements (for example, ROOs), up to 1,600 documents can accompany each truck Shoprite sends with a load that crosses an SADC border. Lack of coordination across government ministries and regulatory authorities also causes significant delays, particularly in authorizing trade for new products. Another South African retailer took three years to get permission to export processed beef and pork from South Africa to Zambia.

In SACU, national protection for infant industries has often been used to justify import bans. Namibia has used the provision to protect a pasta manufacturer and broilers and maintains protective bans on ultra-high temperature (UHT) milk, extending its ban beyond the recently expired eight-year limit for this protection. Botswana has recently limited imports of specific varieties of tomatoes and UHT milk. Seasonal import restrictions on maize, wheat, and flour also ensure that domestic production is consumed first. For example, Swaziland's imports of wheat flour were effectively prohibited for half of 2009, since no import permits were issued since June of that year.

Export taxes also impose costs and inhibit the development of regional supply chains. A case in point is small stock exports from Namibia. Since 2004 the Namibian government has limited exports to encourage local slaughtering. Quantity restrictions were originally used but have recently been replaced by a flexible levy of between 15 percent and 30 percent, effectively closing the border for the export of live sheep to South Africa. The impact of this restriction is affecting the small stock industry in both Namibia and South Africa. In the former, farmers have switched to alternative activities such as cattle and game farming. Those sheep farmers that remain have become almost entirely dependent on the four Namibian export abattoirs, while they were previously able to sell more sheep to the South African market where they received higher prices (PriceWaterhouseCoopers 2007). In South Africa, 975 full-time jobs are at risk because of the scheme, especially in the bigger abattoirs in the Northern and Western Cape that focus on slaughtering Namibian sheep during the low season to better utilize their capacity (Talijaard et al. 2009).

Source: World Bank 2012.

representative of the barriers faced by firms and individuals in crossing borders throughout the continent. These non-tariff barriers impose unnecessary costs on producers and undermine the predictability of the trade regime.

Empirical work on the relationship between export performance and the business environment highlights the importance of this relationship as a constraint on the continent's exports. For instance, regarding time delays in the handling and shipping of merchandise, Djankov, Freund, and Pham (2010) estimate that if Uganda reduced its factory-to-ship time from 58 to 27 days (the median for their sample), exports would be expected to increase 31 percent and Uganda would be closer to its main trading partners by 2,200 kilometers. More recently, using detailed data on different types of delays in customs, Freund and Rocha (2010) examined the impact of the functioning of customs in African nations. In particular, they examine whether delays in transit, delays in documentation, or delays in port handling have significant and differentiated effects on exports. They find that delays in inland transit do have a significant and negative impact on exports. In particular, they find that a one-day reduction in travel time inside the exporting country leads to a 7 percent increase in exports. The other types of delays have a smaller impact on exports.

Beyond overall export performance, the business environment directly affects incentives to enter export markets. Edwards and Balchin (2008) studied in detail the impact of various components of the business environment on the propensity to export in African countries. Using firm-level data from the World Bank's Enterprise Surveys for eight African nations, they generated principal-component indexes to test whether (1) physical infrastructure, (2) micro-level supply constraints, (3) macroeconomic conditions, (4) legal environment, and (5) trade-related infrastructure and services have a significant impact on the propensity to export in these eight African nations.

They found a negative and significant relationship between the propensity to export and the principal components that reflect the following:

- Micro-level supply constraints: This index captures access to land, tax rates and administration, labor regulations, business licensing and operating permits, and the cost of access to financing.
- Unfavorable macroeconomic conditions: The index captures perceptions regarding macroeconomic instability and economic and regulatory policy uncertainty.

- Weak legal environment: This index captures crime and anti-competitive behavior.

Does the business environment affect export survival as well? One might conjecture that once a firm decides that the environment is sufficiently favorable to generate a positive return on exporting—that is, conditional on the decision to enter—survival would not be affected. In fact, one might even expect a negative relationship between the quality of the business environment and average survival. The reason is the selection effect discussed in chapter 1 of this report—namely, that an easier environment may prompt low-productivity, low-quality firms to try to export on a hit-and-run basis, thus reducing export survival averaged over all exporting firms.

Preliminary but direct evidence from a survey conducted in 2009 by the World Bank in five African countries (Ghana, Malawi, Mali, Senegal, and Tanzania) suggests that the quality of the business environment—in particular freight costs, burdensome customs, and corruption—looms large among the factors constraining the ability of African firms to thrive in export markets.

The survey covered both active exporters and those who recently exited export markets, thus potentially singling out factors that dominated the picture for the second category. Figure 2.4 shows the number of respondents mentioning each of a series of possible constraints on survival (out of a menu of 10—multiple responses were allowed) in the form of a scatter plot with the number of respondents among failed exporters (those who exited) on the horizontal axis and the number of respondents among active exporters on the vertical axis.[4] Thus, a constraint factor appearing above the 45° line is revealed as more important to active exporters, while a factor appearing below it is revealed as more important to exited exporters.

Most exporters, whether active or exited, identified freight costs (whether internal or external) as the primary limitation to their expansion (panel a). While in absolute terms this was the answer most marked by both groups of exporters, in relative terms it was more frequent within the group of existing exporters (this result is expected, considering that members of this group are currently dealing with more export transactions than members of the exited group, given their exporting status). The second most frequent answer was "costs and burdensome procedures by customs" in the country of export, followed by "bribes." The relative importance of the most frequent answers is consistent with the evidence in the literature. The frequency with which exporters mention corruption

Figure 2.4   Constraints to Survival

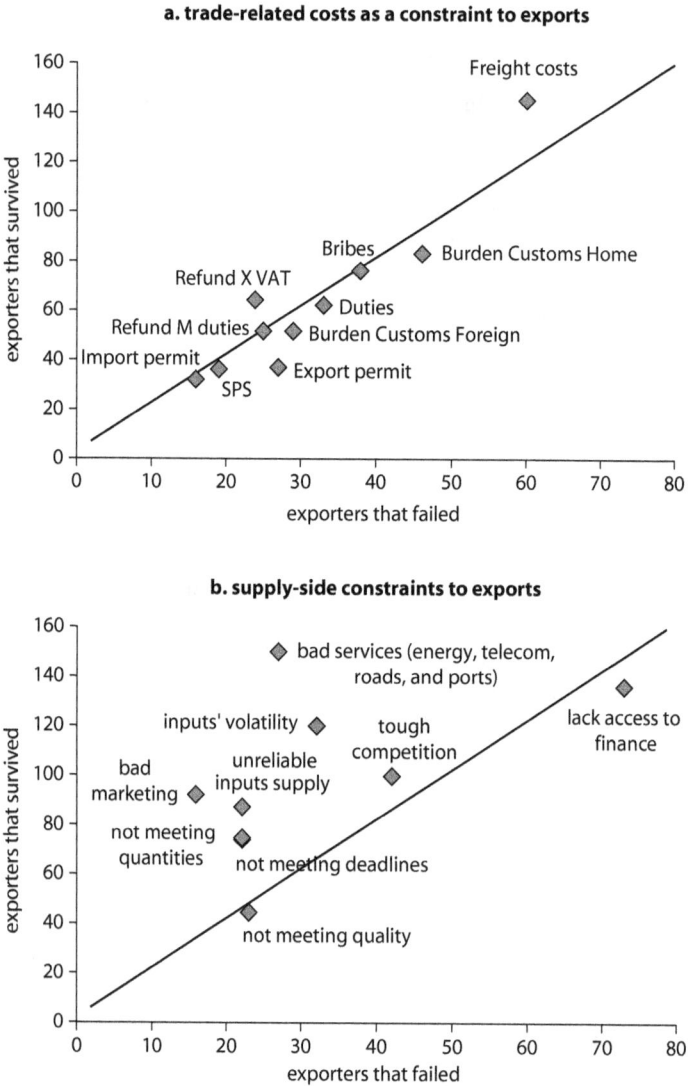

a. trade-related costs as a constraint to exports

b. supply-side constraints to exports

Source: World Bank survey of African exporters, conducted in 2009.
Note: Refund M = refund of import duties; Refund X VAT = refund of export VAT; SPS = sanitary and phytosanitary standards.

as a constraint is particularly important, given that corruption tends to be most damaging to firms that are simultaneously too small to have the connections it takes to go around corrupt officials or tame them, and too large to operate in the less-visible informal market.[5]

Regarding supply-side constraints, exporters were given a menu of nine options covering a wider array of issues (panel b). Access to finance is clearly the major factor identified by both active and exited exporters, suggesting that all exporters, active or failed, hit that constraint—again, this is fully consistent with the empirical literature and with casual observation as well. In absolute terms, bad infrastructure services (mainly representing energy services and port infrastructure) was the most common response marked by the existing exporters. Volatility in input prices and tough competitive behavior from others are the next most marked answers by both groups of exporters.

Using a novel data set of exports at the firm level for countries in Africa, Asia, Eastern Europe, Latin America, and the Middle East, figures 2.5 and 2.6 present more evidence on the relationship of different business environment variables (at the country-year level) and a more direct measure of export survival: first-year export survival rates of new exporters (by country-year).[6]

Export costs per container correlate negatively with export survival, as do delays. Panels a and b of figure 2.5 present the relationship between survival rates and the World Bank's Doing Business indicators of export costs: costs per container and number of days to export. The data for African countries are indicated by triangles. The graphs show a negative relationship between survival rates and these indicators: the lower the export cost and the smaller the delay, the higher the survival rate. This negative relationship is more pronounced in the case of costs per container and is further supported when using a summary measure of trade costs—the Logistics Performance Index (LPI), shown in panel c[7]—which correlates positively, across countries, with export survival. Note that, in all three panels, African countries do not stand out as outliers in terms of low survival. Those lying on the left-hand part of the diagrams, with export costs, delays, and LPIs comparable to those of non-African countries, seem to have, by and large, comparable export survival. What stands out for African countries is not their low survival rates by themselves, but rather the high values of their costs and delays.

Lack of financial development is also an important factor. Figure 2.6 shows the relationship between survival rates and two measures of financial development and structure: private credit of financial institutions to GDP and the value of shares traded in stock market exchange to GDP. These data are taken from the updated version of the New Database on Financial Development and Structure (Beck, Demirgüç-Kunt, and Levine 2000).[8] Overall, there is a positive relationship between survival

Figure 2.5   First-Year Survival Rates and Business Environment Measures in the Origin Country

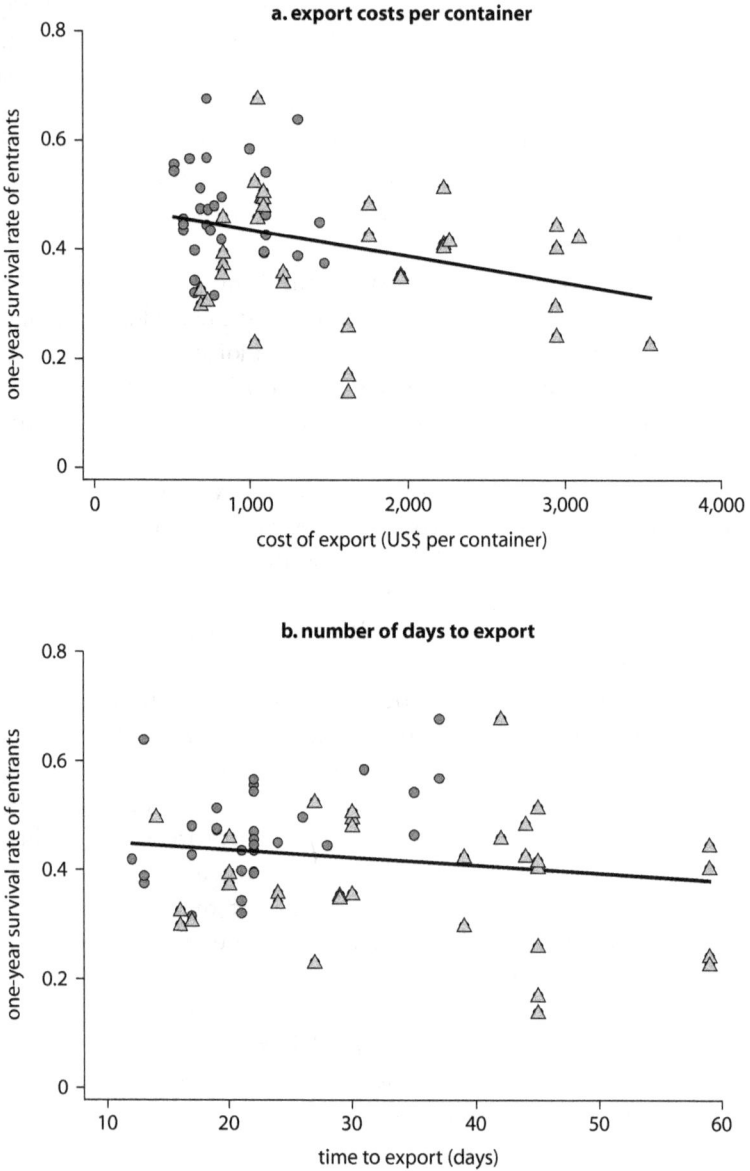

a. export costs per container

b. number of days to export

(continued next page)

Figure 2.5   *(continued)*

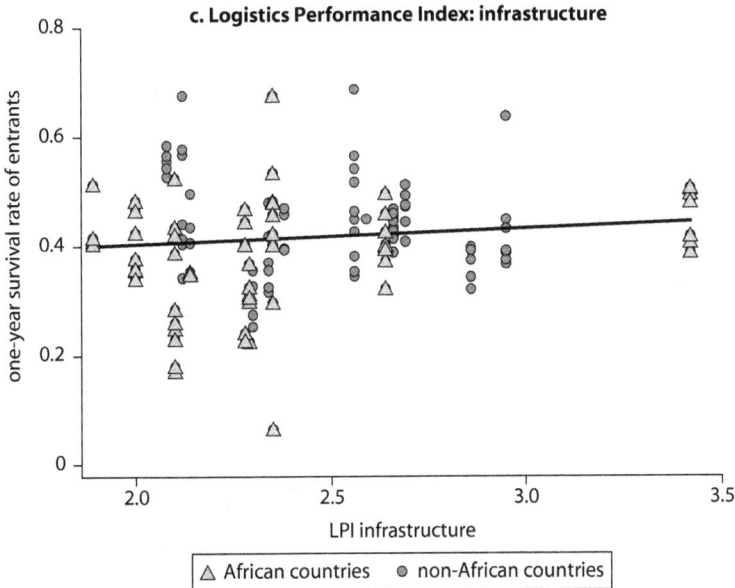

c. Logistics Performance Index: infrastructure

Source: Exporter Dynamics Database (DECTI) forthcoming. Available at: http://econ.worldbank.org/exporter-dynamics-database.

rates and these two variables. Again, most African countries in the sample stand out as being to the left rather than below the regression line, highlighting the explanatory power of these factors in determining the ability of exporters to survive.

Thus, the relationships highlighted in figure 2.6 and the particular patterns they suggest for Africa are consistent with the direct evidence from the survey of exporters—lack of credit and financial development constrains not only entry, but also survival. This can be understood as follows. Often, large-scale buyers in industrial countries "test" new suppliers by ordering limited amounts. When the supplier's performance is satisfactory, the buyer rapidly ramps up orders. It is at this stage that the credit constraint hits the suppliers, who need to invest rapidly to respond to the buyers' scaled-up demands. Ample anecdotal evidence suggests that even with letters of credit and guarantees from reputable buyers—such as supermarket chains in Europe, Japan, or the United States—local banks in Sub-Saharan Africa will refuse to grant credit, or will accept credit applications only with unrealistic collateral requirements and prohibitive interest rates. The supplier will typically not have

Figure 2.6   First-Year Survival Rates and Financial Development

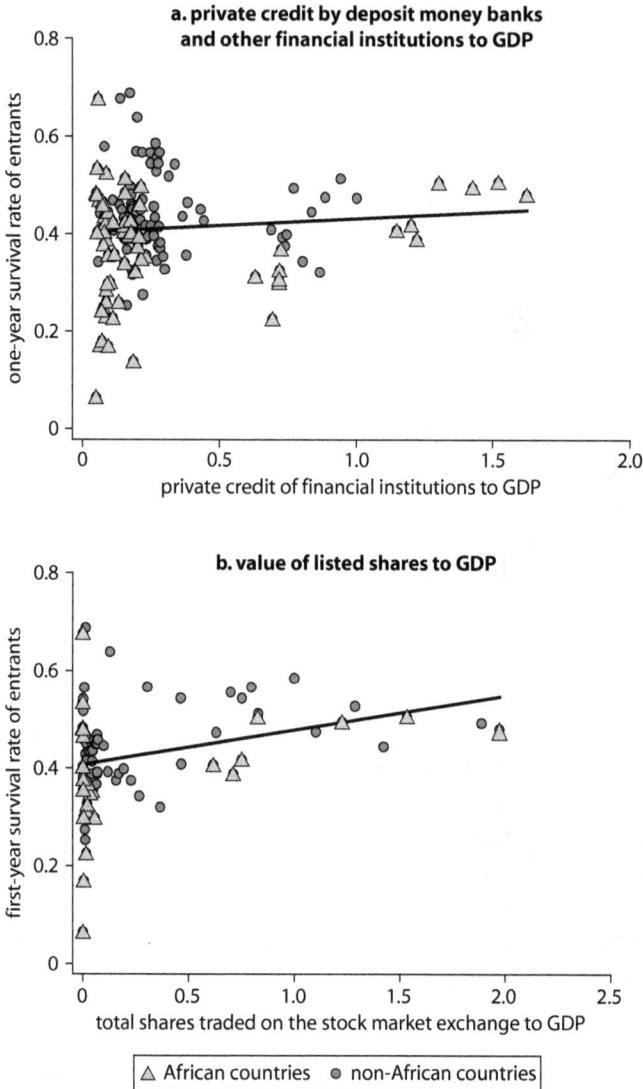

Source: Beck, Demirgüç-Kunt, and Levine 2000.

time to gather the required financing before the buyer switches to alternative sources of supply—e.g., in East Asia, where the supply response is less constrained. The African supplier's inability to ramp up production will thus lead to rapid termination of the export relationship, showing up in the data as low survival—precisely in the sense in which low survival is defined in this section—the ability to survive past the first year.

In order to confirm these findings through formal regression analysis, table 2.1 shows the results of correlations between the variables presented above and survival. All regressions report ordinary least squares results with the unit of observation being the proportion of flows that survive past the first year of export, by product group (Harmonized System [HS] 2-digit level), firm, and destination. The estimations control for the number of entries in order to take into account the selection effect discussed in chapter 1, namely, that an easier environment may induce entry by relatively low performers, thus dampening the induced improvement in average survival rates.

As expected, the number of survivors is highly correlated to the number of entrants in each country-year-HS 2-digit trio, and the squared term also presents a positive and significant relationship.[9] Regarding the business environment variables, after controlling for entry, country, year, and HS 2-digit, we find that only export costs per container are significant in their relationship with survival.

Table 2.1   Survival Versus Business Environment Measures in African Countries: Correlations

	Dependent variable: Log natural (number of surviving entrants)				
	(1)	(2)	(3)	(4)	(5)
Log natural (number of entering firms)	0.328***	0.321***	0.330***	0.490***	0.343***
	(0.0189)	(0.0187)	(0.0162)	(0.0274)	(0.0164)
Log natural (number of entering firms)^2	0.0874***	0.0875***	0.0864***	0.0667***	0.0846***
	(0.00298)	(0.00297)	(0.00262)	(0.00347)	(0.00261)
Log natural (export costs per container)	−0.228***				
	(0.0541)				
Log natural (days to export)		0.130			
		(0.149)			
Private credit by deposit money banks and other financial institutions/GDP			−0.279		
			(0.172)		
Total shares traded on the stock market exchange/GDP				−0.107	
				(0.0705)	
LPI infrastructure					−0.0646
					(0.0507)
Observations	2,534	2,534	3,098	1,188	3,020
R^2	0.94	0.94	0.94	0.97	0.94

Source: Authors.
Note: LPI = Logistic Performance Index
Significance level: *** = 1 percent

This relationship is negative, as expected, indicating that the higher the cost to export, the lower the number of firms that will be able to succeed. In particular, a 10 percent increase in the export costs per container would mean a 2 percent decrease in the number of surviving firms in Africa.

Standards and Their Enforcement

The discussion of the business environment so far has focused largely on trade facilitation, which is crucial for the long-term viability of export businesses in developing countries. Equally crucial is the regulatory environment in destination markets, in particular for agri-food products, to which we now turn. We show, through anecdotal evidence, that African exporters of agri-food products may face considerable discretion and uncertainty on destination markets. Consider the following case study, discussed in Ashraf, Giné, and Karlan (2009).

DrumNet is a program designed by Pride Africa to help small-scale farmers develop long-term business relationships with exporters.[10] The dual problem that DrumNet addresses is that overseas buyers fear that once they provide inputs on credit, farmers will sell their crop to other buyers and refuse to repay their loans; at the same time, farmers fear that buyers will use the exclusive-purchase understanding to "hold them up" and offer low prices for the crop, especially when it is perishable. As a result of this "double moral hazard" problem, farmers do not invest in agricultural improvement or utterly fail to adopt export crops, even when these crops could earn them higher incomes. The DrumNet program aims to build trust between farmers and their buyers and to foster long-term, sustainable business relations between them.

Ashraf, Giné, and Karlan (2009) report the results of a rigorous impact evaluation of DrumNet. They find "positive but not overwhelming one-year impacts" from the program in terms of adoption of export crops and overcoming barriers to market access. However,

> [t]he epilogue to this project is more dismal. One year after the evaluation ended the export firm that had been buying the horticultural produce stopped because of lack of compliance with European export requirements (EurepGap). This led to the collapse of DrumNet as farmers were forced to undersell to middlemen, leaving sometimes a harvest of unsellable crops to rot and thus defaulting on their loans. Afterward it was reported to us anecdotally that the farmers returned to growing local crops (Ashraf, Giné, and Karlan 2009, p. 974).[11]

The incident related by Ashraf, Giné, and Karlan, which illustrates some of the contradictions of industrial countries' development and trade policies, may not be wholly representative in its starkness. However, it points to a real problem—discretion in the administration of sanitary and phytosanitary (SPS) regulations in industrialized countries.

The problem this discretion imposes is better described in the case of the United States by Jouanjean, Maur, and Shepherd (2011). Three federal agencies are involved in the oversight of food safety in the United States: the U.S. Department of Agriculture's Food Safety and Inspection Service (FSIS), the U.S. Food and Drug Administration (FDA), and the U.S. Environmental Protection Agency (EPA). The FSIS ensures the safety of imported meats, poultry, and processed egg products. The FDA covers all other products. The EPA licenses pesticide products and monitors pesticide residues in products. The FDA enforces compliance with limits on pesticides residues, food hygiene, additives, and contamination.

Under Section 801 of the Federal Food, Drug and Cosmetics Act (FD&C), products are subject to inspection when imported. Imported food products are expected to meet the same standards as domestic products; in addition, since 1997 fruit and vegetable producers must follow the FDA's good agricultural practices (GAP) for the control and management of microbial food safety. Likewise, since 1995 imported fish products must meet hazard analysis and critical control point (HACCP) standards, as must domestic producers. In the United States, HACCP standards apply to processors only, in contrast to the European Union, where they apply to the entire supply chain (see below). Other measures applying to seafood include traceability requirements such as the identity preservation system for mollusks, and labeling of origin and method of production (wild harvest or farm-raised).

All the measures described above are in accordance with the principle of national treatment, as they apply equally to importers and domestic producers. There is, however, a significant difference: The FD&C Act allows for the rejection of imported FDA-regulated products for "appearing" to be adulterated or misbranded. According to Jouanjean, Maur, and Shepherd (2011),

> The law is interpreted in a broad sense as allowing the FDA to make admissibility decisions based not only on physical evidence such as examination, facility inspection, or laboratory results, but also based on historical data, information from other sources (e.g. about a disease outbreak), labeling, and any other evidence. . . . Factors such as reputation can clearly come into play in this decision. In other words, if there is the faintest suspicion that a

product from a given origin will not meet FDA standards, it can be detained. Therefore the standard of proof for determination of refusal for food import products is much less strict than for domestic products, which must be based on an actual violation (Jouanjean, Maur, and Shepherd 2011, p. 9).

Such a discretionary regime is bound to generate periodic sales disruptions for exporters and—perhaps more important for African producers—to overpenalize those who are climbing up the quality ladder because their history weighs on them. It thus creates uncertainty of the kind that was shown in annex 1A of chapter 1 to have negative effects on survival, both direct (unanticipated termination) and indirect (discouragement effect making exporters less resilient to bad news).

Beyond discretionary regimes, the evolution of standards in destination countries can put gradual pressure on exporters in low-income countries in a way that threatens their sustainability, pushing them to adopt deep changes in the structure of value chains as survival strategies and making it very difficult for smaller players to survive in the tougher regulatory environment.

Senegal's exports of French beans, studied in detail by Maertens and Swinnen (2009) and Jaud and Cadot (2011), is a case in point. EU standards for fresh fruit and vegetables (FFV) have been steadily rising, putting enormous pressure on exporters. EU legislation imposes (1) common marketing standards for FFV; (2) SPS; (3) general hygiene rules based on HACCP control mechanisms', and (4) traceability standards. These measures became notably more stringent in the 1990s. Particularly relevant to FFV is reduced tolerance for chemical residue levels.[12] First, about 350 active substances initially approved for use in the European Union have been gradually withdrawn (out of the 823 initially allowed). Second, Maximum Residue Levels (MRL),[13] as well as import tolerances (ITs),[14] are imposed at levels specific to particular protection chemical–crop combinations. The registration of an IT is a complicated process involving the submission of a complete residue dossier, including field trials and lab analysis results. For exporters of minor crops—most tropical crops except bananas—from developing countries, the challenge is compounded by the fact that agrochemical companies have little incentive to provide registration residue data for those crops because the benefit would not cover the cost.

The HACCP and traceability requirements came into force with the General Food Law of 2002 (EC/178/2002). Traceability means that EU food companies must document from (to) whom they are buying (selling) so that products can be traced back to their origin if they prove defective or dangerous. Although traceability is legally limited to a "one step forward, one step back" principle within the European Union (with no obligation to keep records in third countries), in practice EU buyers tend to go beyond the strict legal requirement. Complete traceability throughout the chain all the way up to the overseas producers is part of many private standards such as those of the GlobalGAP.

Maertens and Swinnen's analysis shows that the European Union's rising standards have profoundly altered the structure of the supply chain in Senegal's horticulture sector. For instance, the financial constraints generated by the need to comply with increasingly stringent standards have induced consolidation at the intermediation stage, with only the larger firms able to cope. Between 2002 and 2005, the number of French bean exporters dropped from 27 to 20, and the market share of the three largest companies rose from less than half to two-thirds (Maertens and Swinnen 2009).

Rising standards have complex implications for export survival and risk-sharing along the value chain, as the overall sector's sustainability as a supplier to the increasingly regulated market can be obtained by shifting risk over to the producers upstream. In the case of Mali's mango exports, for instance, complete traceability all the way up to the farmer comes with precise tracking of quality records. Farmers that are recorded to have supplied less than 60 percent of "export-grade" mangoes during a specified period are automatically tossed out of the supply chain (see box 2.2), notwithstanding the fact that every single mango shipment is screened for

Box 2.2

A Malian Mango's "Soldier's Run"

In order to reach EU markets, a mango must be patient, tough, and spotless. The run starts with a manual sorting that eliminates fruits with visible defects and those that have lost their peduncle, which would allow moisture to infiltrate them. Those fruits that survive the first sorting are immersed for 5 minutes in a 50° pool in order to eliminate insects and anthracnose risk. A second, 2-minute immersion in prochlorase—a bacteria-killing detergent—further reduces infection risk. After drying, a new round of selection eliminates all fruits bearing any trace of cochineal. Cochineal contact involves no health risk for consumers, but traces might possibly put them off, and the retailers will take no chances. The second round of selection

(continued next page)

Box 2.2 *(continued)*

is followed by calibration, which is necessary to condition the fruits in cardboard boxes subjected to very strict weight restrictions. The calibration team's work is then verified by another team; any errors send the fruits back to the previous stage. Finally, each box is stamped with a seven-digit traceability code identifying the conditioning station, the week of conditioning, the day of the week, and the lot. Lot identification includes reference to a producer ticket, thus guaranteeing total traceability. The producer ticket identifies the name of the collector, the village of origin, the producer's name, the land plot number, the date of harvest, and the number of cages or containers containing the mangoes supplied by the producer.

Boxes are piled on wood pellets and then stored in a cold-storage facility at 9°, with a temperature sensor put in one of the fruits for constant monitoring. They are then shipped by refrigerated truck, and then by truck, rail, and cargo ship via Abidjan (during the troubled period in Côte d'Ivoire, they were shipped by an alternative route that included rail transshipment at Ferkessedougou, which involved several days of inland transit). The sea journey usually takes 12 days with the best shipping lines, and can take up to 20 days, which makes the supply chain very tight, given that the life of a mango typically does not exceed 28 days. The fruits may also be shipped by air freight, but that makes them very expensive, given their weight.

Fruits that were rejected from the export supply chain end up on the local market with a substantially marked-down price. The conditioning unit tracks the "export-grade" ratio of each producer—that is, the ratio of fruits that make it to the total supplied by that producer. This ratio must hover around 60 percent, with a tolerance around +/–10 percent. When a producer's ratio dips below this tolerance, he is tossed out of the supply chain. Thus, the supply chain's survival is, at least in part, the result of the fact that the risk of failing its extraordinarily strict requirements is largely pushed up the chain, to the farmers. In that sense, the sustainability of the export flow and income security of the producers may even be inversely correlated.

Source: Cadot 2008.

defects and non–export grade fruits are thrown away or sold locally. Thus, the price for the sector's survival is the shifting over of the survival risk onto farmers. The resulting uncertainty does not appear in the product-level statistics, since the overall flows are not affected; nor does it even appear in the firm-level statistics that can be gathered from customs administrations, as the firms appearing in those statistics are the intermediaries, not the ultimate producers. Yet it is not something that should be glossed over, as the risk is unlikely to be fully diversifiable or insurable at the household level.

In the case of Senegal, this tension between sustainability at the sector level and individual risk for farmers has given rise to new contractual and market-structure arrangements. First, the relationship between intermediaries and producers has changed, so there is now more control by intermediaries over farming methods. Tighter control was implemented through increasingly precise contracts, technical assistance, and the provision of credit and farm inputs. Second, the induced changes also affected the structure of upstream farm production, with a sharp decrease in the incidence of contract farming and a rise in that of large-scale estate production. Maertens and Swinnen show, from data from a survey they conducted in Senegal's French bean–producing region, that the share of agricultural households that took part in export production through contract farming dropped from 23 percent in 2000 to less than 10 percent in 2005, whereas the share of households that had at least one member working as a salaried employee on a plantation rose in the same period from 10 percent to 34 percent. Interestingly, Maertens and Swinnen show that these transformations have been accompanied by reductions in the incidence of extreme poverty. However, there are no data on the effect of these transformations on the *volatility* of income, which is one of the key potential effects of low export survival.

Overall, this chapter shows the following:

- A poor business environment—in particular, high trade costs—is associated with lower rates of export survival. This suggests that government interventions that seek to promote the export of particular products may have little impact in the face of a hostile business environment and a high rate of export failure. We return to policy implications later in the report.
- Discretionary application of trade and regulatory policies in overseas markets increases uncertainty about market access and so has negative impacts on export survival. This chapter gives the example of standards in Western markets but applies equally to standards applied in Africa and other developing-country markets, as well as to policy instruments such as rules of origin and periodic import and export bans.
- The impact of higher standards is complex, but such standards can lead to a shift of risk within export value chains to poor producers in developing countries and affect survival possibilities for particular suppliers.

Annex 2A: Survey of African Exporters on Export Survival

The objective of the Survey of African Exporters on Export Survival was to obtain information from both successful exporters and firms that have exited from export markets on specific factors that, in their opinion, affected their ability to survive and thrive in foreign markets.

This survey was conducted in 2009 in five African countries: Ghana, Malawi, Mali, Senegal, and Tanzania. The sample of exporters who participated in this survey was randomly drawn from the total population of exporters in each country, based on their customs data. The preestablished criteria taken into account to draw the sample of exporters were

- exporting status of the firm,
- its size,
- its location, and
- the economic sector in which it operates, at the 2-digit level of the Harmonized System (HS) Code.

In particular, all the exporters in each country were classified into four groups according to their exporting status in 2008, the last year covered by the customs data available at that time for these four countries: (1) *regular exporters* are those exporters with consecutive exports until 2008; (2) *past exporters* are the exporters who were exporting consecutively for at least two years and then exited the market permanently before 2008; (3) *intermittent exporters* are those who exported erratically during the period included in the sample; and finally (4) *new exporters* are those exporters who appear for the first time in the sample in 2008.

Over 200 firms were contacted in each country. However, because of low cooperation and identification problems with some of the firms, the final sample by country and exporting group was the following:

Table 2A.1   Survey of African Exporters on Export Survival: Distribution of Exporters by Exporter Type

Country	Intermittent	New	Past	Regular	Total
Ghana	6	4	37	65	112
Malawi	9	13	15	54	91
Mali	12	18	20	48	98
Senegal	28	24	31	39	122
Tanzania	22	8	16	38	84
Total	77	67	119	244	507

Source: Authors.

The questionnaire administered during this survey contained basic questions about the firm and questions about specific factors affecting the survival of the exporters and potential opportunities for exporters' expansion. Regarding general information about the characteristics of the firms interviewed, the answers to the first question of the questionnaire reveal the following:

- Sixty-eight percent of the firms are domestically owned, 27 percent are foreign owned, and 5 percent have mixed or other type of ownership.
- Although the vast majority of the participating managers have pursued undergraduate or graduate studies (78 percent), the proportion of responding managers who had only elementary or high school education was higher among the group of exporting companies that had exited the market before 2008 (39 percent of all responding managers within this group).
- The share of managers who are male within the entire group of respondents was an overwhelming 92 percent.
- Only 21 percent of the responding managers revealed that they had received training from the Export Promotion Agency.
- Almost a third (30 percent) of the participating managers responded that their exporting company operated in an Export Processing Zone.

Regarding the specific factors affecting survival, the following two questions were asked:
On trade costs:

Are any of the following costs relating to exporting a constraint to the expansion of your sales abroad?

1. Costs related to complying with sanitary, phytosanitary, and technical regulations?   Yes ☐ No ☐
2. Costs that arise from delays and burdensome procedures in home customs?   Yes ☐ No ☐
3. Costs that arise from delays and burdensome procedures in customs abroad?   Yes ☐ No ☐
4. Difficulties and costs in getting an export permit or license?   Yes ☐ No ☐
5. Difficulties and costs in obtaining an import permit abroad?   Yes ☐ No ☐

6. Duties in markets abroad higher than expected?   Yes ☐ No ☐

   If "Yes," is this due to:

   6.1. Inability to get tariff preferences the company
        is eligible for?   Yes ☐ No ☐

   6.2. Authorities in the export market do not
        accept company's certificate of origin?   Yes ☐ No ☐

   6.3. Difficulties with customs in the overseas
        market regarding valuation of the export or
        its classification?   Yes ☐ No ☐

   6.4. Unexpected changes in the tariff on the
        company's main product(s)?   Yes ☐ No ☐

7. High costs of freight to the export market?   Yes ☐ No ☐

8. Difficulties in getting refund of import duties on
   imported inputs that the company is eligible for
   under a duty drawback scheme?   Yes ☐ No ☐

9. Difficulties in getting refund of VAT on exports
   for which the company is eligible?   Yes ☐ No ☐

10. Problems with unforeseen payments to officials?   Yes ☐ No ☐

11. Was there another important factor not mentioned
    above?   Yes ☐ No ☐

On supply-side costs:

Regarding specific supply constraints **(in addition to the export costs covered in the previous question)**, are any of the following a constraint to the expansion of the exports of your company?

1. Unreliability of input supply?   Yes ☐ No ☐

2. Volatility of input prices?   Yes ☐ No ☐

3. Problems in meeting the buyers' requirements
   regarding quality?   Yes ☐ No ☐

4. Problems in meeting deadlines to deliver the
   product to the buyer?   Yes ☐ No ☐

5. Problems in providing the quantities requested by
   the buyer?   Yes ☐ No ☐

6. Inability to access the finance necessary to support
   the export activity?   Yes ☐ No ☐

6.1. Lack of finance limits the expansion of the
company's production to a larger scale   Yes ☐   No ☐

6.2. Lack of finance limits the investment into
improving the products' quality   Yes ☐   No ☐

7. Competition that undermines your company's
ability to export?   Yes ☐   No ☐

8. Problem with key services inputs (such as energy,
telecom, etc.)?   Yes ☐   No ☐

If "Yes," what is the main problem?

8.1. Energy?   Yes ☐   No ☐
8.2. Telecommunications?   Yes ☐   No ☐
8.3. Roads?   Yes ☐   No ☐
8.4. Ports?   Yes ☐   No ☐

9. High costs of marketing abroad?   Yes ☐   No ☐

10. Was there another important factor not
mentioned above?   Yes ☐   No ☐

The answers to these questions are presented and discussed in the scatter graphs of figure 2.4 in this chapter.

Notes

1. The database of Revealed Factor Intensity Indices (RFII) is available in Excel and Stata format at http://r0.unctad.org/ditc/tab/research.shtm and has recently been updated to 2007. A complete description of the original database can be found in Tumurchudur, Shirotori, and Cadot 2006.

2. In interpreting this result, one should keep in mind that in a Heckscher-Ohlin-Vanek model with more goods than factors, the underlying framework for the revealed factor intensities constructed by UNCTAD—since it uses 5,000 products, based on the classification of products at the 6-digit level of the Harmonized System (HS) and only three factors of production—trade patterns are formally indeterminate (unlike in a two-good, two-factor framework). Trade flows are only *correlated* with factor intensities.

3. Preliminary results by Nicita, Shirotori, and Tumurchudur-Klok (2011) suggest, however, that this effect may be temporary.

4. The detail of the questions asked to exporters during this survey can be found in annex 2A.

5. In this case, most of the responding firms that indicate corruption as their main constraint are located in the bottom third of the size distribution of firms in the sample for this survey.

6. The first-year survival rates of entrants, in each country, were calculated as the ratio of the number of firms that enter in year t (so they were not present in year $t-1$) and survived at least until year $t+1$ over the total number of firms that entered in year t. The data contained in these graphs cover the following 23 countries: Burkina Faso, Cameroon, Kenya, Mali, Mauritius, Malawi, Niger, Senegal, Tanzania, Uganda, and South Africa from Africa; Cambodia and Pakistan from Asia; Albania and Bulgaria from Eastern Europe; Chile, Colombia, Costa Rica, the Dominican Republic, Ecuador, Mexico, and Peru from Latin America; and Jordan from the Middle East. The coverage in terms of years varies per country, although only three cases have data before 2000 (Costa Rica, Mexico, and Peru); in most cases, reliable data are available only from 2005 onward. Source: Exporter Dynamics Database (DECTI)

7. The Logistic Performance Index (LPI) for infrastructure is a measure of perceptions of the quality of physical infrastructure. This number indicates a score between 1 and 5, where 1 is the worst possible scale of performance and 5 is the best. See http://go.worldbank.org/88X6PU5GV0.

8. See http://go.worldbank.org/X23UD9QUX0.

9. We use the product-related information from the Database on Export Growth and Dynamics at the HS 2-digit because of its availability at the time when these regressions were estimated.

10. Pride Africa is a nongovernmental organization founded in 1988. Its first activity consisted of developing microfinance schemes in Kenya, after which it expanded into other Sub-Saharan African countries and into a general model of business franchises whose objective is to encourage local entrepreneurship. DrumNet started in 2004 in Kenya as one such franchise, designed to deliver services to agro-buyers, banks, farm input retailers, and farmers. It developed over time into a full program. See http://www.prideafrica.com.

11. EurepGap, which was made mandatory in January 2005, is part of the good agricultural practices (GAP) protocol of the Euro-Retailer Produce Working Group (EU-REP), a group of EU supermarkets.

12. In the late 1990s, an updated harmonized legislation package on pesticide Maximum Residue Limits (MRL)—EC Directive 91/414 and subsequent Regulation 396/2005—created concern for African, Caribbean, and Pacific horticultural exporters because of its stringency.

13. The MRL is the level of residue legally permitted to remain in/on a food or animal feedstuff following the use of a crop-protection chemical (CPC) under good agricultural practice (GAP)—that is, under the specific label instructions of the approved product.

14. An *import tolerance* is an MRL set for imported products containing active plant-protection substances not authorized in the European Union for reasons other than public health, or when a different level is appropriate because the existing Community MRL was set for reasons other than public health.

References

Albornoz, Facundo, H. F. Calvo Pardo, G. Corcos, and E. Ornelas. 2010. "Sequential Exporting." CEP Discussion Papers dp0974, Centre for Economic Performance, LSE.

Alvarez, Roberto, and R. Lopez. 2005. "Exporting and Firm Performance: Evidence from Chilean Plants." *Canadian Journal of Economics* 38: 1384–400.

Araujo, Luis, and E. Ornelas. 2007. "Trust-Based Trade." CEP Discussion Papers dp0820, Centre for Economic Performance, LSE.

Ashraf, Nava, X. Giné, and D. Karlan. 2009. "Finding Missing Markets (and a Disturbing Epilogue): Evidence from an Export Crop Adoption and Marketing Intervention in Kenya." *American Journal of Agricultural Economics* 91: 973–90.

Aw, Bee Yan, and A. Hwang. 1995. "Productivity in the Export Market: A Firm-Level Analysis." *Journal of Development Economics* 47: 313–32.

Baldwin, John R., and W. Gu. 2003. "Export-Market Participation and Productivity Performance in Canadian Manufacturing." *Canadian Journal of Economics* 36: 634–57.

Beck, Thorsten, A. Demirgüç-Kunt, and R. Levine. 2000. "A New Database on Financial Development and Structure." *World Bank Economic Review* 14: 597–605.

Bernard, Andrew B., J. Eaton, J. B. Jensen, and S. Kortum. 2003. "Plants and Productivity in International Trade." *American Economic Review* 93: 1268–90.

Bernard, Andrew B., and J. B. Jensen. 1995. "Exporters, Jobs, and Wages in U.S. Manufacturing: 1976–1987." *Brookings Papers on Economic Activity: Microeconomics* 67–119.

———. 1999. "Exceptional Exporter Performance: Cause, Effect, or Both?" *Journal of International Economics* 47: 1–25.

———. 2004. "Why Some Firms Export." *Review of Economics and Statistics* 86: 561–69.

Bigsten, Arne, P. Collier, S. Dercon, M. Fafchamps, B. Gauthier, J. W. Gunning, A. Oduro, R. Oostendorp, C. Pattillo, M. Söderbom, F. Teal, and A. Zeuf. 2004. "Do African Manufacturing Firms Learn from Exporting?" *Journal of Development Studies* 40 (3): 115–41.

Bigsten, Arne, and M. Söderbom. 2006. "What Have We Learned from a Decade of Manufacturing Enterprise Surveys in Africa?" Policy Research Working Paper 3798, World Bank, Washington, DC.

Blalock, Garrick, and P. Gertler. 2004. "Learning from Exporting Revisited in a Less Developed Setting." *Journal of Development Economics* 75: 397–416.

Boermans, Martijn. 2010. "Learning-by-Exporting and Destination Effects: Evidence from African SMEs." Unpublished. Hogeschool Utrecht University of Applied Sciences. Available at SSRN: http://ssrn.com/abstract=1612770 or http://dx.doi.org/10.2139/ssrn.1612770.

Brambilla, Irene, D. Lederman, and G. Porto. 2010. "Exports, Export Destinations, and Skills." NBER Working Paper 15995, National Bureau of Economic Research, Cambridge, MA.

Cadot, Olivier. 2008. "Stratégie de Développement Commercial, Rapport de cadrage." Unpublished report. Bamako: Rapport pour le Gouvernement du Mali.

Cadot, Olivier, C. Carrère, and V. Strauss-Kahn. 2011. "Export Diversification: What's Behind the Hump?" *Review of Economics & Statistics* 93: 590–605.

Cadot, Olivier, L. Iacovone, D. Pierola, and F. Rauch. 2011. "Success and Failure of African Exporters." Policy Research Working Paper 5657, World Bank, Washington, DC.

Castellani, Davide. 2002. "Export Behavior and Productivity Growth: Evidence from Italian Manufacturing Firms." *Review of World Economics* 138: 605–28.

Clerides, Sofronis, S. Lach, and J. Tybout. 1998. "Is Learning by Exporting Important? Micro-Dynamic Evidence from Colombia." *Quarterly Journal of Economics* 113 (3): 903–47.

Collier, Paul, and J. W. Gunning. 1999. "Explaining African Economic Performance." *Journal of Economic Literature* 32: 64–111.

Crozet, Matthieu, K. Head, and T. Mayer. 2009. "Quality Sorting and Trade: Firm-Level Evidence for French Wine." CEPII Working Paper 2009–14, CEPII, Paris.

Damijan, Joze P., S. Polanec, and J. Prasnikar. 2004. "Self-Selection, Export Market, Heterogeneity and Productivity Improvements: Firm Level Evidence from Slovenia." LICOS Discussion Paper 14804, Katholieke Universiteit, Leuven.

De Loecker, Jan. 2004. "Do Exports Generate Higher Productivity? Evidence from Slovenia." LICOS Discussion Paper 151, Katholieke Universiteit, Leuven.

Delgado, Miguel A., J. Farinas, and S. Ruano. 2002. "Firm Productivity and Export Markets: A Non-Parametric Approach." *Journal of International Economics* 57: 397–422.

Djankov, Simeon, C. Freund, and C. Pham. 2010. "Trading on Time." *The Review of Economics and Statistics* 92 (1): 166–73.

Dutt, Pushan, I. Mihov, and T. van Zandt. 2008. "Trade Diversification and Economic Development." Unpublished. INSEAD, Fontainebleau, France. http://faculty.insead.edu/dutt/Research/diversification.pdf.

Eaton, Jonathan, M. Eslava, M. Kugler, and J. Tybout. 2008. "Export Dynamics in Colombia: Firm-Level Evidence." In *The Organization of Firms in a Global Economy*, ed. E. Helpman, D. Marin, and T. Verdier, 231–72. Cambridge, MA: Harvard University Press.

Edwards, Lawrence, and N. Balchin. 2008. "Trade-Related Business Climate and Manufacturing Export Performance in Africa: A Firm-Level Analysis." *Journal of Development Perspectives* 4 (1): 67–92.

Freund, Caroline, and N. Rocha. 2010. "What Constrains Africa's Exports ?" Policy Research Working Paper 5184, World Bank, Washington, DC.

Girma, Sourafel, D. Greenaway, and R. Kneller. 2004. "Does Exporting Increase Productivity? A Microeconometric Analysis of Matched Firms." *Review of International Economics* 12: 855–66.

Graner, Mats, and A. Isaksson. 2007. "Firm Efficiency and the Destination of Exports: Evidence from Kenyan Plant-Level Data." Unpublished document. UNIDO. http://www.unido.org/fileadmin/user_media/Publications/Pub_free /Firm_efficiency_and_destination_of_exports.pdf.

Greenaway, David, and R. Kneller. 2007. "Firm Heterogeneity, Exporting and Foreign Direct Investment." *The Economic Journal* 117: 134–61.

Hagemejer, Jan, and M. Kolasa. 2008. "Internationalization and Economic Performance of Enterprises: Evidence from Firm-Level Data." MPRA Working Paper 8720, Munich.

Hansson, Par, and N. Lundin. 2004. "Exports as Indicator on or as Promoter of Successful Swedish Manufacturing Firms in the 1990s." *Weltwirtschaftliches Archiv* 140: 415–45.

Harding, Alan, M. Söderbom, and F. Teal. 2004. "Survival and Success among African Manufacturers." CSAE Working Paper Series 2004–05, Centre for the Study of African Economies, University of Oxford, Oxford.

Hausmann, Ricardo, and D. Rodrik. 2003. "Economic Development as Self Discovery." *Journal of Development Economics* 72: 603–33.

Hausmann, Ricardo, J. Hwang, and D. Rodrik. 2007. "What You Export Matters." *Journal of Economic Growth* 12: 1–25.

Heritage Foundation. 2011. Index of Economic Freedom (database). http://www .heritage.org/index/default.

Jaud, Mélise. 2011. "Food Safety, Reputation, and Trade." Working Paper halshs-00586310, HAL Paris School of Economics, Paris.

Jaud, Mélise, and O. Cadot. 2011. "A Second Look at the Pesticides Initiative Program: Evidence from Senegal." Policy Research Working Paper 5635, World Bank, Washington, DC.

Jouanjean, Marie-Agnes, and O. Cadot. 2011. "A Second Look at the Pesticides Initiative Program: Evidence from Senegal." Policy Research Working Paper 5635, World Bank, Washington, DC.

Jouanjean, Marie-Agnes, J.-C. Maur, and B. Shepherd. "US SPS Enforcement: Do Refusals Harm Reputation?" Forthcoming in *Non-Tariff Measures: New Analysis for Trade Policy's New Frontier*, ed. O. Cadot and M. Malouche. London/Washington, DC: The World Bank and CEPR. (Center for Economic and Policy Research).

Levchenko, Andrei. 2007. "Institutional Quality and International Trade." *Review of Economic Studies* 74: 791–819.

LPI (the Logistics Performance Index). Database. World Bank, Washington, DC. http://go.worldbank.org/88X6PU5GV0.

Maertens, Miet, and J. Swinnen. 2009. "Trade, Standards, and Poverty: Evidence from Senegal." *World Development* 37 (1): 161–78.

Mayer, Thierry, M. Melitz, and G. Ottaviano. 2011. "Market Size, Competition, and the Product Mix of Exporters." Working Papers 2011-11, CEPII research center.

Melitz, Marc. 2003. "The Impact of Trade on Intra-industry Reallocations and Aggregate Industry Productivity." *Econometrica* 71: 1695–725.

Mengistae, Taye, and C. Pattillo. 2004. "Export Orientation and Productivity in Sub-Saharan Africa." *IMF Staff Papers* 51 (2): 327–53.

Naumann, Eckart. 2008. "Intra-SADC and SADC-EU Rules of Origin: Reflections on Recent Developments and Prospects for Change." Draft. TRALAC, Stellenbosch.

Nicita, M. Shirotori and B. Tumurchudur-Klok. 2011. "Survival Analysis of LDCs' Exports: The Role of Comparative Advantage." Unpublished document. UNCTAD, Geneva.

Nunn, Nathan. 2007. "Relationship Specificity, Incomplete Contracts, and the Pattern of Trade." *Quarterly Journal of Economics* 122: 569–600.

Pisu, Mauro. 2008. "Export Destinations and Learning-by-Exporting: Evidence from Belgium." NBB Working Paper 140, National Bank of Belgium, Brussels.

PriceWaterhouseCoopers. 2007. "Evaluation of the Implementation of the Small Stock Marketing Scheme in Relation to the Namibian Government's Value Addition Goals and Objectives." Windhoek: PriceWaterhouseCoopers.

Schott, P. 2003. "One Size Fits All? Heckscher-Ohlin Specialization in Global Production." *American Economic Review* 93: 686–708.

Talijaard, P., Z. Alemu, A. Joote, H. Jordaan, and L. Botha. 2009. "The Impact of Namibian Small Stock Marketing Scheme on South Africa." National Agricultural Marketing Council, South Africa.

Tewari, Meenu. 1999. "Successful Adjustment in Indian Industry: The Case of Ludhiana's Woolen Knitwear Industry." *World Development* 27: 1651–71.

Tumurchudur Klok, Bolormaa, M. Shirotori, and O. Cadot. 2010. "Revealed Factor Intensity Indices at the Product Level." Policy Issues in International Trade and Commodities Study Series No. 44, UNCTAD, New York and Geneva.

Van Biesebroeck, Johannes. 2003. "Exporting Raises Productivity in Sub-Saharan Manufacturing Plants." NBER Working Paper 10020, National Bureau of Economic Research, Cambridge, MA.

Volpe, Christian, and J. Carballo. 2009. "Survival of New Exporters in Developing Countries: Does It Matter How They Diversify?" IDB Working Paper WP-I140, Inter-American Development Bank, Washington, DC.

Wagner, Joachim. 2002. "The Causal Effect of Exports on Firm Size and Labor Productivity: First Evidence from a Matching Approach." *Economics Letters* 77: 287–92.

———. 2007. "Exports and Productivity: A Survey of the Evidence from Firm-Level Data." *World Economy* 30: 60–82.

World Bank. Ease of Doing Business. Website. World Bank, Washington, DC. http://www.doingbusiness.org/.

———. Enterprise Surveys. Website. http://www.enterprisesurveys.org/.

———. 2010a. *Doing Business 2011: Making a Difference for Entrepreneurs.* Washington, DC: World Bank.

———. 2010b. "Connecting to Compete: Trade Logistics in the Global Economy. The Logistic Performance Index and Its Indicators." World Bank, Washington, DC.

———. 2011. "Facilitating Cross-Border Trade between the DRC and Neighbors in the Great Lakes Region of Africa: Improving Conditions for Poor Traders." Report No. 62992-AFR, http://siteresources.worldbank.org/INTAFRREGT OPTRADE/Resources/Great_Lakes_Final_Report_21_June_11.pdf.

———. 2012. *De-Fragmenting Africa: Deepening Regional Trade Integration in Goods and Services,* P. Brenton and G. Isik, ed. Washington, DC: World Bank.

CHAPTER 3

Survival, Contracts, and Networks

In chapter 2, we analyzed some of the determinants of export sustainability at the country level—mainly comparative advantage, the business environment, and standards and technical regulations. In this chapter, we further evaluate the determinants of survival by assessing the links between survival and firm strategies and informal institutions, primarily discussing the role of linkages and networks.

Exports, Firms, and Survival

The survival of an export spell and that of the exporting firm are linked by the simple fact that if the firm ceases to exist, so will the products that it exports. However, there is more than this to the relationship, as exit from export markets can be a survival strategy for the exporting firm—getting out of money-losing markets may be part of a strategic repositioning or restructuring process. Thus, exit from export markets may reflect either the firm's exit from business or a decision to cut losses that conditions its survival. The following section provides a brief overview of the empirical literature on firm exit decisions, looking for possible linkages to export survival.

What Do We Know about Firm Survival?

Beyond the simple observation above, the literature is largely silent on the relationship between export survival and firm survival. However, some indirect inferences can be made from the literature on firm exit decisions, especially those of multinational firms. The gist of the argument is that exporting firms are typically stronger than non-exporting ones, so firm exit is unlikely to be a key differential driver of short export survival, although it may, of course, contribute somewhat. Instead, the most frequent reason for the exit of an export spell from a product-origin-destination combination is likely to be a managerial decision to shift outlets for a given production facility or to move that production facility to a different location.

Exporting firms are typically larger and more productive than non-exporting ones (see, among others, Bernard et al. 2007). By the same token, they are also stronger and able to survive longer. Firm attributes that correlate with survival also correlate with the decision to export. For instance, Audretsch and Mahmood (1995); Audretsch, Santarelli, and Vivarelli (1999); Disney, Haskel, and Heden (2003); Dunne, Roberts, and Samuelson (1988); and Mata and Portugal (1994) find that firm characteristics such as productivity, capital intensity, wage levels, and size correlate with survival. We already saw that these characteristics correlate with the decision to export. Thus, because exporting firms are the largest and most productive firms, they are also the best equipped to survive, and the high turnover observed in export activities *cannot* be primarily explained by a particular vulnerability of exporting firms. If anything, exporting firms are stronger than non-exporters; therefore, a substantial part of the observed churning has to be caused by voluntary decisions to exit export markets because costs are too high or profitability is too low—in other words, because export markets are particularly tough.

Export-oriented investments by multinational companies in labor-intensive sectors might be conjectured to contribute to improve average export survival in the host country, because these companies are likely to be among the strongest. However, that may well not be the case, because they are also footloose. In one of the early papers, Flamm (1984) showed that multinationals hedge against local country risk by spreading production sites over several locations even when doing so entails higher costs (his object of study is semiconductor assembly, which is highly labor-intensive and uses largely unskilled entry-job female labor). By reducing cross-location switching costs, multinationals make their production facilities footloose. Easy switching reduces sunk costs. While in the model presented in annex 1A of chapter 1 uncertainty was found in the export market, in Flamm's model uncertainty emanates from the production site. However, the logic remains the same. With lower sunk costs of entry and exit (an easier switching of production from one site to another), multinationals make themselves less willing to put up with losses on the production site, contributing to shorter export spells. Maintaining a diversified portfolio of production sites induces multinationals to keep several sites active at all times, but the location of those sites may shift around.

Later studies confirmed that multinationals were more footloose than domestic firms after controlling for firm and industry differences (Bernard and Sjöholm 2003; Görg and Strobl 2003b; Girma and Görg 2004), although Mata and Portugal (2002) and Özler and Taymaz (2007) found no significant difference in survival rates between domestic and multinationals. Ferragina, Pittiglio, and Reganati (2011) found substantial variation across sectors on Italian data. All in all, the literature suggests that export-oriented investment by multinationals does not appear to be, in itself, necessarily conducive to better export survival.

The literature surveyed so far has not uncovered a strong causal link between patterns of firm or plant closure and patterns of exit from export markets or from a particular product-origin-destination combination. In fact, causation may run the other way around. Bernard and Jensen (2002, 2007) showed that the probability of firm exit decreases with the number of products produced and the number of markets served. Thus, exporting and export diversification, in particular when this diversification takes place into several geographical markets, enhances firm survival, either through hedging of risk or through better access to inputs.

Could it be, however, that firm survival correlates negatively with export survival at the product-origin-destination cell level? As the diversification of production facilities, in Flamm's argument, makes multinationals footloose, one might expect that simultaneously operating in different cells might make firms more willing to close one and open another, making expected survival lower at the firm-cell level. Volpe and Carballo (2009) and Cadot et al. (2011) find the opposite pattern—namely, that a firm-cell's survival correlates *positively* with the number of markets the firm serves with that product and with the number of products that it ships to the same destination. Low-income countries have mainly single-product, single-market exporters, whereas in middle-income countries there are more multi-product, multi-market exports.

Thus, diversification does not make firms footloose across cells and does not explain churning. Quantitatively, in Volpe and Carballo (2009), adding one destination does as much as adding three products on survival; in Cadot et al. (2011), it does as much as adding six products. These results are confirmed by Carrère and Strauss-Kahn's 2011 study. Looking at spell survival on Organisation for Economic Co-operation and Development (OECD) markets, they find that one non-OECD destination—for the same origin-product pair at the Standard International Trade Classification (SITC)-5 level—adds 11 percentage points to the probability of first-year survival, from 35.7 percent to 46.8 percent, while a second destination adds another 6 percentage points. To have the same effect on survival, the range of products exported to the same destination would have to shoot up from the [0–30] bracket to the [30–200] bracket.[1]

Contracts, Reputations, and Trade Relationships

Incomplete enforcement of contracts across borders affects export survival in two ways: (1) by inducing termination of relationships when one party reneges on a contract and (2) by reducing transaction volumes, which, as we saw earlier, correlate with survival.

International trade is particularly vulnerable to incomplete contract enforcement. In the words of Dani Rodrik:

> Transaction costs [in international trade] arise from various sources, but perhaps the most obvious is the problem of contract enforcement. When one of the parties reneges on a written contract, local courts may be unwilling—and international courts unable—to enforce a contract signed between residents of two different countries. Thus national sovereignty interferes with contract enforcement, leaving international transactions hostage to an increased risk of opportunistic behavior (Rodrik 2000, p. 179, quoted in Araujo and Ornelas 2007).

In the presence of incomplete contract enforcement, market mechanisms typically emerge to alleviate moral hazard and adverse selection. Moral hazard is typically dealt with through self-enforcing contracts with credible non-legal sanctions (later in this chapter, we will discuss the role of ethnic and other networks in this regard), while adverse selection is typically dealt with through signaling and the building of reputations.

Reputations are built in the course of repeated interaction. In the case of producers located in developing countries, empirical evidence suggests that buyers in industrial countries typically first test them through small orders, and then ramp up transaction volumes upon satisfactory performance in the pilot-order phase. Sometimes, small volume is the choice of the exporter himself. Tewari (1999) cites the case of an Indian knitwear exporter who was approached by JCPenney for large orders and turned down the offer, preferring to stick with a small-scale business relationship with Ferrucci and other Italian buyers.

> JCPenney promised big orders, but very low rates. The European firms were small; they gave small orders but the rates were better, and they had built up a relationship with us. They gave advice, and the small orders made it possible [for us] to learn from our mistakes (Rai Bahadur interview, 1990, 1998, cited in Tewari 1999, pp. 1663–64).

As Tewari further discusses, learning at the firm level typically takes place in small steps, which means that the "one mistake and you are out" environment of the supply chains manned by volume retailers is hardly those where reputations could be built progressively.

These insights have been formalized by Rauch and Watson (2003) in a theoretical model showing that buyers who are uncertain about the capabilities of their suppliers start relationships with small orders, and then ramp up transaction volumes. Their model shows that the initial "underordering" is more severe when the cost of searching for new partners increases. It also shows that large-volume transactions correlate with longer persistence. The reason is that both correlate with lower costs. We saw in annex 1A of chapter 1 that the higher the profitability is of an export business, the more the exporter will persist during bad times. Similar reasoning applies to buyers: the lower the supplier's cost, the higher the transaction's profitability. This will raise both volumes purchased and persistence. The positive relationship between transaction volumes and the reputation of the party with uncertain quality or moral hazard is also found in Araujo and Ornelas (2007) and Jaud (2011).

Learning and Synergies

If firms do not learn from exporting, it does not matter how long they stay in export markets: high churning does not deprive them from dynamic economies of scale. But if firms learn from exporting, keeping them in the market is important, because exiting has an opportunity cost that goes beyond the lost sales. Put another way, the learning effect might well be what drives the decreasing hazard rates observed in some of the empirical work on survival. That is, give exporters time to learn and they will figure out how to survive. We will see in this section whether the empirical literature offers any guidance on how to maximize learning effects, the lessons of which may be relevant for policies to raise survival rates.

If there are synergies between exporters, the dynamic learning effect is compounded by a market failure—namely, the positive externality that exporters exert on each other. Intuitively, it is not obvious why exporters should reinforce each other: one would rather expect them to compete with each other. But channels of interaction other than price—which is unlikely to be a strong one for small-scale African exporters anyway—may exist, whereby exporters reinforce each other's credibility. The following two sections will explore these conjectures in turn.

Do African Firms Learn from Exporting?

Whether firms learn from exporting or simply self-select into exporting markets when they are more efficient has been a subject of controversy for a while in the international trade literature. Exporters are typically the upper tail of the distribution of firms in terms of size, capital intensity, productivity, wage levels, and survival (see, for example, Bernard and Jensen, 1995, 1999, 2007). Until recently, the weight of the empirical evidence supported the theoretical insight initiated by Melitz (2003): that more efficient firms exported because they were more efficient, not the other way around, because learning effects appeared small or insignificant. Most of the papers in this strand of literature (Aw and Hwang 1995; Castellani 2002; Delgado, Farinas, and Ruano 2002; Hansson and Lundin 2004; Wagner 2002) used data from industrial countries, which means that their applicability to an African context was limited. But a few used data from developing countries. Clerides, Lach, and Tybout (1998) used data from Colombia and Mexico; Isgut (2001) from Colombia; and Alvarez and Lopez (2005) from Chile, all with pretty much the same message.

More recently, however, new empirical evidence has emerged suggesting that firms do learn from exporting, in particular when they operate from emerging markets. Most of this literature relies on matching techniques.[2] Blalock and Gertler (2004) found that the total factor productivity (TFP) of Indonesian exporters rose more than that of non-exporters. De Loecker (2004) and Hagemejer and Kolasa (2008) also found that exporting firms had larger TFP growth than matched non-exporting ones.

More relevant to us, Bigsten et al. (2004), Graner and Isaksson (2007), and Mengistae and Pattillo (2004) found support for the learning-by-exporting hypothesis in terms of various performance measures including TFP growth on various samples of Sub-Saharan African manufacturing firms in the 1990s.

How can we reconcile these two strands of conflicting evidence? First, the new literature's interpretation of learning-by-exporting is fairly wide. Papers in this strand identify transformational processes including, in particular, capital deepening. They also identify performance improvements including higher sales, earnings, and employee salaries, but none of these changes constitutes direct evidence of "learning" in the strict sense, even though they may well go with learning by managers and employees. There is no direct evidence, for instance, of exporting firms organizing or participating in training programs.[3] There is also little guidance from the theoretical literature. Albornoz et al. (2010) propose a model in which firms learn about the profitability of export, which is correlated over time within destinations and across destinations as well. Entry generates information that firms use to revise their profitability expectations for future entry and exit decisions. The model suggests that firms are more likely to exit a destination market after one year when that year is their first try, because information is then minimal. As firms accumulate experience over export spells and markets, they become less sensitive to bad news. Thus, in Albornoz et al., learning is a reduction in uncertainty about key parameters, not an improvement in production processes.

Some anecdotal evidence on the channels through which learning-by-exporting takes place can be found in the literature on cross-border supply chains. Rhee, Ross-Larson, and Pursell (1984) described, in their classic survey of manufacturers from the Republic of Korea (a survey carried out in 1975, at a time where Korea was still a relatively poor country), how technology was transferred by foreign buyers to their suppliers:

> The relations between Korean firms and the foreign buyers went far beyond the negotiation and fulfillment of contracts. Almost half the firms said they had directly benefitted from the technical information foreign buyers provided: through visits to their plants by engineers or other technical staff of the foreign buyers, through visits by their engineering staff to the foreign buyer, . . . (Rhee, Ross-Larson, and Pursell 1984, p. 61; quoted in Rauch 2001).

Gereffi (1999) also described how least-developed-country producers of textile and apparel products producing under CMT ("cut, make, and trim," meaning assembly of clothing products with precut pieces of fabric) typically learn how to source fabric themselves and produce to the buyer's design, progressively transforming themselves into branded manufacturers. The anecdotal evidence is thus suggestive of learning through the interaction that takes place between buyers and subcontractors in global value chains. There is little evidence, even anecdotal, of learning through arms-length relationships. The lack of evidence does not imply that learning does not take place either, however—it means simply that we do not know whether it does or does not.

A second issue is that the two literatures referred to above describe different things. The earlier one draws mainly from samples of firms located in industrial or middle-income countries, whereas the later one uses samples of firms from developing countries. One may thus conjecture that the scope for learning-by-exporting somehow relates to the exporter's distance from the technological frontier. The more backward a firm's technology and management culture are (as proxied by the income level of the origin country), the more that firm can learn from contact with demanding buyers located in higher-income markets.

Indeed, a number of papers have identified "destination effects" whereby firms exporting to higher-income countries appear to differ in both characteristics and production methods from those exporting only to lower-income ones. Crozet, Head, and Mayer (2009); Damijan, Polanec, and Prasnikar (2004); Graner and Isaksson (2007); and Pisu (2008), among others, all find evidence of destination effects. Brambilla, Lederman, and Porto (2010) use the Brazilian devaluation of the 1990s as a natural experiment to identify destination effects on Argentine firms. They do find that, as firms redirected their sales away from the less-profitable Brazilian market toward higher-income destinations, they became more skill-intensive in a way that is measurable at the firm level. Mengistae and Pattillo (2004) also find that exporting to non-African markets generates stronger improvements in performance measures than exporting solely within Africa. Using the World Bank's Regional Program on Enterprise Development (RPED) survey of manufacturing firms located in five Sub-Saharan African countries, Boermans (2010) finds evidence of learning-by-exporting and of destination effects. That is, those exporters with sales outside of Africa report a higher capital intensity; they also report, upon starting to export, higher increases in employment and earnings than matched control firms.[4]

As in the case of learning-by-exporting, we do not know much about the channels through which destination effects take place. It may be that selling to demanding markets induces transformational changes in exporting firms, possibly with technical assistance from buyers (see our previous discussion on food standards). Alternatively, Mayer, Melitz, and Ottaviano (2011) have developed a model showing how tougher competition in a destination market—reflected in lower markups on all products sold on that market—induces firms to concentrate on their best-performing products in that market. They also provide supporting evidence from French firms. Thus, it may be that the improvement in performance measures is a composition effect within the firm (across products) rather than a transformation of *all* production processes.

All in all, it is fair to say that the weight of the evidence is increasingly on the side of the existence of learning economies (dynamic economies of scale) in exporting, particularly for producers in poor countries that may start far away from the efficiency frontier. These learning economies can interact with survival in two ways: (1) learning makes exporters stronger over time (higher TFP and earnings), which contributes to their ability to survive; and (2) reducing the infant mortality of exports can be expected to have two effects: a direct one (reducing the number of exits) and an indirect one (giving exporters access to a second phase of life where hazard rates are lower).

Synergies

Synergies between exporters can take several forms. First, exporters' decisions to enter foreign markets and their subsequent success or failure may reveal information about the parameters of demand on those markets and the capabilities (costs and productivity) of similar producers from the same country to serve that demand. In that way, exporters help the "self-discovery" process discussed by Hausmann and Rodrik (2003). Second, they may—if one believes the learning-by-exporting hypothesis discussed in the previous section—adopt new processes and products that allow them to better survive in foreign markets. These "discoveries" may be imitated by other firms, making those imitating firms also better able to enter and survive in foreign markets. Third, there may be "critical mass" effects. When a sufficiently large number of firms serve a given market with a given product, they may get noticed by buyers who will then interpret signals in a more favorable way. Likewise, the presence of several firms in a product-destination niche may help convince bankers in the origin country that there is business potential, which may ease access to finance for each one of the exporting firms.

In one of the first papers exploring synergies, Clerides, Lach, and Tybout (1998) tested for spillovers from exporting by including an industry-level export-intensity index as one of the explanatory variables in firm-level export-participation and cost functions. A significant effect on the participation function would signal externalities on the cost of entry—consistent with the "self-discovery" conjecture—and a significant effect on the cost function would signal externalities on production processes. Results were disappointing—effects on both the probability of entry and costs were imprecisely estimated, partly because the industry-level externality variable was highly collinear with the exchange rate and sometimes went the wrong way, leading the authors to conclude that there might even be crowding out via factor markets.

Closer to our concerns here, Cadot et al. (2011) tested directly for cross-exporter externalities on the ability to survive using a firm-level data set of exporters from four African countries.[5] Their performance variable is the probability of surviving past the first year at the level of a (firm × product × destination) cell. Controls include the number of products the same firm exports to the same destination, the number of destinations to which the same firm exports the same product, the export spell's initial value, and the product's share in the firm's overall exports. The regression also includes time and origin-destination effects. Synergies across exporters are measured by the number of firms from the same origin exporting the same product to the same destination—direct national competitors. Their point estimate implies that, for example, doubling the number of national competitors at the cell level, from 22 to 44, would raise the first-year survival probability of a Senegalese firm from 22 percent to 26 percent. This effect is highly significant, although quantitatively limited.

What is the source of the cross-exporter synergy? There is no direct evidence on information spillovers. Audretsch (1991) and Doms, Dunne, and Roberts (1995) relate innovation to firm survival, so products and process improvements may be one of the things that firms steal from each other when they operate in similar markets. Beyond conjecture, the World Bank survey of African exporters already discussed in chapter 2 can be used to get a glimpse at information sharing on one dimension—contacting buyers. Figure 3.1 shows that competitors' networks are mentioned as the primary source of contacts with clients by only 15 percent of the survey's African respondents, coming after "third party"—a

Figure 3.1   Source of Client Contact, 2009

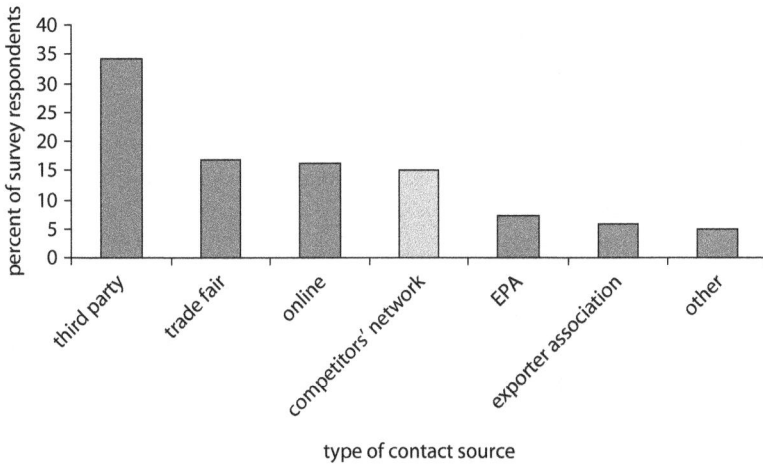

Source: World Bank survey of African exporters, conducted in 2009.
Note: EPA = Economic Partnership Agreement.

catch-all category—but also trade fairs (17 percent) and online research (16 percent).

Thus, direct informational spillovers do not appear as a driving force of the synergy identified. Cadot et al.'s (2011) preferred hypothesis is, instead, the presence of indirect spillovers operating via the banking system. Consider the following scenario. A Senegalese firm is approached by a U.S. buyer to provide a small trial order of t-shirts. Upon successful delivery and sale, the buyer is satisfied and again contacts the Senegalese firm for a larger order. Now the Senegalese firm has to ramp up capacity and, for that, it needs support from financial institutions. In Sub-Saharan Africa, financial institutions may not take letters of credit from the buyer at face value, because they are aware of the risk of all sorts of glitches—quality or others—that may appear down the line. In fact, anecdotal experience suggests that the bank's response will typically be "no" irrespective of the proofs of profitability that the exporter shows, and the trade relationship with the U.S. buyer will end before it had a chance to bear fruit. However, if several Senegalese firms already sell t-shirts on the U.S. market, the same financial institutions may be more easily convinced about the chances of success of this venture and better evaluate the potential risks involved in this transaction.

If this scenario is representative, the synergy effect should be stronger for products that are highly dependent on external finance, because initial financial constraints would be more binding on those sectors. Cadot et al. (2011) test this conjecture by interacting their synergy variable with the measure of dependence on external finance proposed by Rajan and Zingales (1998).[6] The interaction term is positive and significant, suggesting that, indeed, synergies are stronger for finance-dependent products. As an alternative way of getting a handle on the degree of dependence from finance, Cadot et al. (2011) use a proxy for "asset tangibility" proposed by Braun (2003).[7] The idea is that firms with more tangible assets present lower risks because these assets provide real guarantees for bank loans, and information asymmetries (adverse selection or moral hazard) are less important with good collateral, so synergy effects should play a lesser role. The interaction of asset tangibility with the synergy effect has a negative and significant coefficient, implying that firms belonging to industries with high asset tangibility (essentially these are capital-intensive industries) are less sensitive to the synergy effect.

Networks: Migrants and Diasporas

In this section we discuss the effect of migrants and diasporas on export survival, with special attention given to the role they play in the African continent.

Networks and Trade

Networks, whether based on kinship, ethnic groups, or city-states, are as old as trade itself. Greif (1989, 1993) provides a detailed description, based on historical records, of the eleventh-century Maghribi Jewish traders' network in the Arab-dominated Mediterranean. The literature conjectures that traders' networks serve essentially two functions:

- provide information to members about market opportunities and risks and facilitate the matching of buyers and sellers (see, for example, Rauch and Casella 2003).
- overcome moral hazard through various informal incentive mechanisms.

There is plenty of anecdotal evidence in support of both conjectures (see Rauch 2001 for a complete review of the literature). As for information,

Saxenian (1999), for instance, argued that the development of software exports from southern India was linked to the existence of a network of Indian immigrant entrepreneurs in the United States. As for moral hazard, Cohen (1971) showed how the Hausa, a network of ethnically related traders with roots in northern Nigeria, organized its diaspora in Ibadan (a city in Yoruba land, in southwest Nigeria) to enforce obligations among members:

> Among the Hausa, the creditworthiness of a business landlord is measured first by his housing assets. He cannot dispose of these assets without the mediation of the chief of his community. The chief also acts as arbitrator in business disputes. A landlord cannot sell his houses overnight and leave the community after embezzling the money of traders. On the other hand, when it is necessary, the Chief can put a great deal of pressure on a landlord in difficulties to sell some of his housing assets in order to meet his financial obligations to traders (Cohen 1971, p. 274).

In this case, network relations are not the only mechanism for contract enforcement: the cultural tradition of accumulating wealth through an illiquid asset—land—makes community-based contract enforcement easier, although ultimately there is no court-based or other hard enforcement mechanism. Similarly, in their study of Chinese networks of traders abroad, Weidenbaum and Hughes (1996) note, "If a business owner violates an agreement, he is blacklisted. This is far worse than being sued, because the entire Chinese network will refrain from doing business with the guilty party" (p. 51, cited in Rauch 2001).

The bonds that hold diasporas together go well beyond business relations. Cohen (1971) stresses particularly the role of religion in West Africa:

> Islam has been associated with long-distance trade in West Africa because it provided a blue-print for the establishment of networks of communities. . . . [T]o the extent that it has been interconnected with trade, it has done so not as an epiphenomenon, but as the blue-print of a politico-economic organization which has overcome the many basic technical problems of the trade. Indigenous traders become Moslems in order to partake in the moral community of other traders. In both Ibadan and Freetown, nearly half the population are Christians. Yet in both cities all the butchers without any exception have converted to Islam, because only in this way can they participate in the chain of trade in cattle which extends from the savannah down to the forest area (Cohen 1971, pp. 277–78).

Quantitatively, the effect of diasporas on international trade flows has been estimated by including stocks of migrants in gravity equations. Gould (1994) estimated one-way trade to and from the United States using gravity determinants as well as the stock of migrants from each of the partner countries in the United States. He found that a 10 percent increase in the stock of migrants from a given origin country raised that country's exports to the United States by 8.3 percent. Performing a similar exercise for Canada, Head and Ries (1998) found somewhat smaller but also significant elasticities, with a 10 percent increase in the stock of migrants from a partner country, raising that country's exports to Canada by 3.3 percent.

Gravity estimates are largely black boxes. Rauch and Trindade (2002) tried to disentangle the two conjectures mentioned earlier about the function of networks by running separate gravity equations for differentiated products versus reference-priced ones, following Rauch's definition, using ethnic Chinese population shares in 57 countries for 1980 and 1990. They conjectured that if networks helped essentially in matching buyers with sellers, the effect would be stronger for differentiated products, for which matches are harder because of the heterogeneity of the products, than for reference-priced ones. They found that the effect of Chinese diasporas in trading countries had a significant positive effect on bilateral trade worldwide for both types of products, but more for differentiated ones, providing support for the informational-role (matching) hypothesis. Interestingly, they also found that the effect shrunk in magnitude between 1980 and 1990, raising the issue of whether improved access to information could reduce the importance of networks. This is surely the case with the generalization of Internet access.

In sum, recent research on trade and networks suggests that they provide both better information and alternative mechanisms for contract enforcement in weak legal environments. In the case of African exporters, these mechanisms are of interest for several reasons. First, low-income exporters are often assumed to suffer from difficult access to information. However, figure 3.2 shows that, according to the World Bank's survey of African exporters previously mentioned, marketing difficulties are not perceived, by the respondents' own account, as an important constraint to exporters' expansion, especially compared with access to credit (the first concern) and port, customs, and logistics (the second).

Second, African exports to developing countries with low levels of legal security may be affected by moral hazard, which may be alleviated

Figure 3.2   Importance of Barriers to Export: Regular Exporters (Number of Responses), 2009

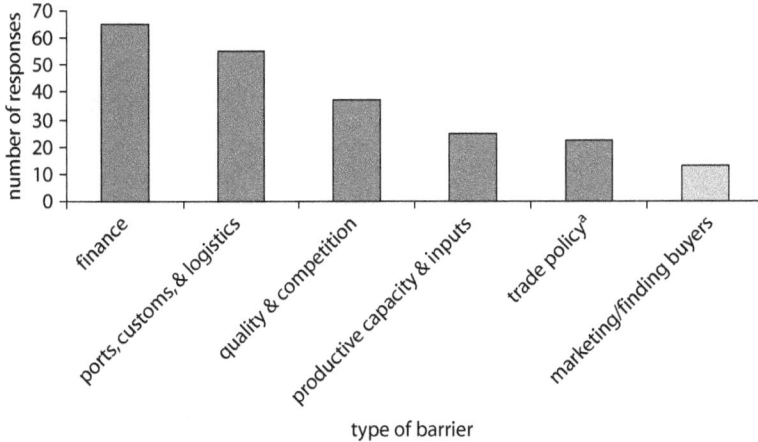

Source: World Bank survey of African exporters, conducted in 2009.
a. Trade policy is composed of tariffs, taxes, procedures, and regulations.

by the presence of local diasporas. In order to explore these conjectures more formally, we first turn to some stylized facts about African migrations within and outside of the continent.

African Migration Patterns

African migration patterns have varied considerably over the last 30 years as a result of conflicts and violent disruptions, but a constant feature is the relatively high proportion of intra-African migration—precisely the result of local disruptions. However, this high proportion of intra-African migration is not reflected in enhanced levels of intra-African trade flows, at least not through formal channels. Overall migration patterns are shown in table 3.1. These patterns are strikingly skewed, with South-North migrations largely dominating the picture, a majority of zeroes, and only a few nonzero flows to southern destinations, including those from Africa to the Middle East.

Table 3.1 has important implications for our conjectures on the role of migrant diasporas. The bulk of the diasporas are to high-income countries, which are generally characterized by high levels of legal security. Thus, one might think that the scope for informal enforcement mechanisms described in the previous section might be limited. However, the transaction costs of litigation in high-income countries are high, and access to

Table 3.1   Origin and Destination of Emigrant Stocks by Region
percent of total emigration

			Destination				
Origin	Africa	East Asia & the Pacific	Europe & Central Asia	Latin Am. & the Car.	Middle East	South Asia	High-income countries
Africa	**50**	0	0	0	**4**	0	**46**
East Asia & the Pacific	0	15	0	0	1	0	83
Europe & Central Asia	0	0	59	0	0	0	41
Latin America & the Caribbean	0	0	0	13	0	0	87
Middle East	2	0	1	1	45	0	51
South Asia	0	2	0	0	8	30	61
High-income countries	1	1	3	5	2	0	87

Source: Ratha et al. 2011.

complex legal systems may not be easy for relatively inexperienced immigrant-entrepreneurs or for small-scale traders with relatively low-level business disputes. Thus, even in high-income environments, informal dispute-resolution and contract-enforcement mechanisms may be efficient.

Intra-African migration patterns are shown in table 3.2. With the exception of North Africa, which essentially migrates outside of the continent, migration patterns are heavily intra-regional, especially for West and southern Africa. This reflects cultural proximity, to some extent, but also the incidence of forced migration. According to Ratha et al. (2011), 2.2 million Africans live as refugees in countries other than their own because of wars and natural disasters.

As of end-2009, the main refugee groups were located in Chad, the Democratic Republic of Congo, Kenya, and Sudan, which together "hosted" about a million refugees. The main origins of refugees were the Democratic Republic of Congo, Eritrea, Somalia, and Sudan, which together account for about 1.8 million refugees (Ratha et al. 2011). These emigrant stocks are likely to be too vulnerable, impoverished, and enclaved to serve as trade facilitators.

What do we know about individuals who migrate and their households? The World Bank's Living Standards Measurement Surveys, together with surveys carried out in Burkina Faso, Nigeria, and Senegal

Table 3.2   Origin and Destination of Emigrant Stocks by African Region, Percent of Total Emigration

Origin	North Africa	Central Africa	East Africa	Southern Africa	West Africa	Out of continent
			Destination			
North Africa	6	0	0	0	0	93
Central Africa	0	23	26	9	3	39
East Africa	3	1	52	3	0	41
Southern Africa	0	0	7	66	0	28
West Africa	0	5	0	0	71	24

Source: Ratha et al. 2011.

as part of the World Bank's Africa Migration Project, provide some information. Unsurprisingly, larger households are more likely to send one member into emigration. Income and education seem to have, at least to some extent, opposite effects. An educated head of household makes emigration by at least one member of the household more likely; for instance, in Ghana, an additional year of education for the head of a household raises the probability of emigration by one household member by 8 percent (Ratha et al. 2011). However, past a certain level, income rises make emigration less likely. These may reflect the positive effect of education on access to information needed for emigration and the negative effect of local opportunities associated with income on the incentive to move. Survey results for Burkina Faso, shown in figure 3.3, highlight the occupational changes that go with migration.

The fact that the majority of the respondents were farmers before migration is due to sample selection, as the survey was administered in rural areas. Keeping this caveat in mind, the survey highlights interesting occupational changes, in particular for internal migrants, among whom the proportion of farmers drops from 85.7 percent to 36.4 percent, whereas the proportion of traders—the case that is most interesting in terms of effects on trade—rises from 4.5 percent to 20.9 percent. Among international migrants, however, occupational changes are—surprisingly—smaller, with the proportion of traders rising only from 2.4 percent to 6.8 percent. The rise in the proportion of professionals is much larger, from 2.1 percent to 23 percent. This may reflect a better ability of migrants to leverage their level of education in environments where the demand for skills is higher than in their area of origin.

These stylized facts highlight a complex picture in which emigration reflects highly diverse incentives—voluntary or not—and where networks

Figure 3.3   Occupational Changes of Internal and International Migrants: Burkina Faso, 2009

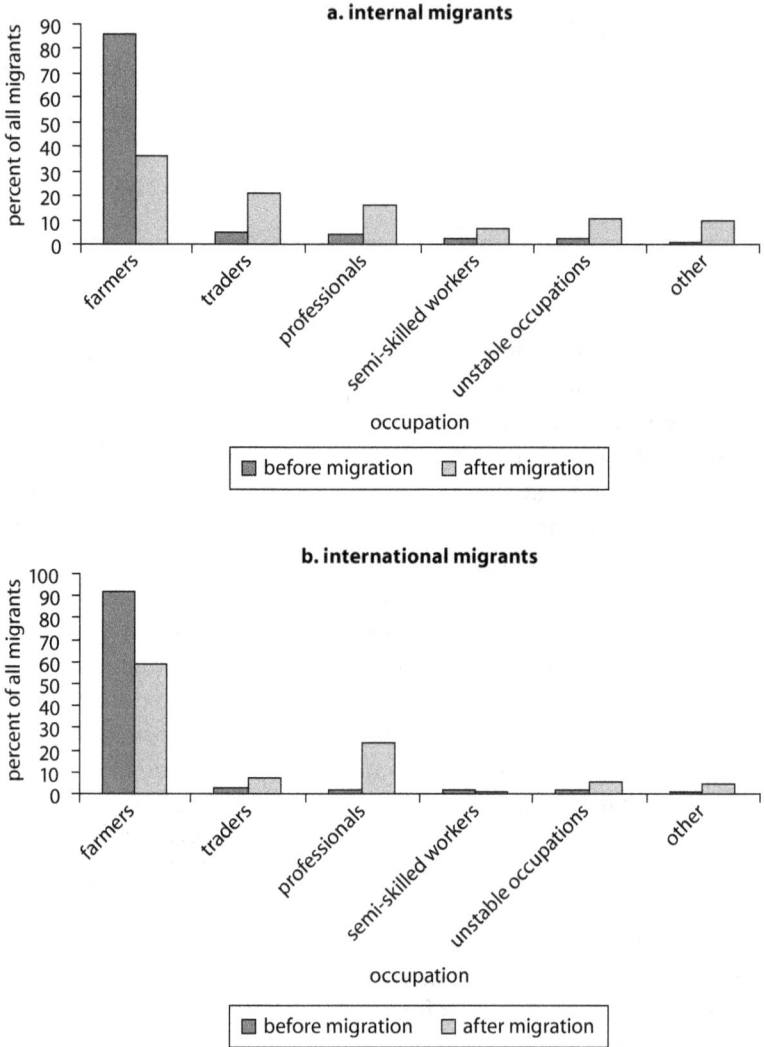

a. internal migrants

b. international migrants

Source: Ratha et al. 2011.

of traders such as the eleventh-century Maghribi or today's Nigerian Hausa or Chinese diasporas may, actually, be fairly rare among African migrants. These should serve as caveats for the analysis of the effect of migrations on the survival of exports, which we consider next.

Migrants, Diasporas, and Export Survival

We now turn to a quantitative exploration of the relationship between export-spell survival and migrant stocks in destination countries based on the large set of export spells used in chapter 1. We modified this data set in order to make it compatible with our migration data. Bilateral (origin-destination) migrant stock data are from the World Bank and include two waves of migration measurement: 1990 and 2000. Accordingly, we kept only those spells that started in 1990 and 2000 and attributed to each one the relevant bilateral migrant stock evaluated in the corresponding year. This, of course, sharply reduced the number of observations to little more than 61,000.

Control variables include the log of the spell's initial dollar value, the growth of its value during its lifetime, a dummy variable marking multiple spells, and a number of typical gravity variables. These include, for both origin and destination countries, the dollar value of GDP (in logs); landlockedness dummies; import and export costs, in U.S. dollars per container; distance; common language, border, and colonial history; and exchange-rate volatility. The justification for including gravity-type variables in a survival regression follows annex 1A of chapter 1. Results are shown in table 3.3. The three specifications differ only by the inclusion of migration variables, shown in the second part of the table.

Results are largely in line with expectations. Large initial spell values correlate with lower hazard rates. Spell value growth, however, and multiple spells correlate with higher hazard rates. Although the coefficient on spell value growth is unintuitive, the coefficient on multiple spells is to be expected since both multiple spells and higher hazard rates mean more stop-and-go in the export relationship. Coefficients on gravity variables are in line with the predictions of the simple model in annex 1A of chapter 1. Exporter and importer income levels correlate with lower hazard rates. Landlocked exporters have higher hazard rates, which may reflect both the mechanisms highlighted in the model and also the fact that land routes may be more susceptible to sudden disruptions. The variables on proximity (common border, language, and colonial past) have unintuitive coefficients, where exchange-rate volatility has a very small effect.

Migration variables have effects that are largely in line with the discussion above. The stock of exporter country migrants in the importer country (EMIC) correlates negatively with hazard rates. This result supports the hypothesis that migrant networks contribute to overcome moral hazard in trade relationships. The stock of migrants from the

Table 3.3 Export-Spell Hazard Rate Estimates: Cox Regressions

	(1)	(2)	(3)
Spell attributes			
Initial spell value	−0.0811***	−0.0842***	−0.0843***
	(0.00236)	(0.00236)	(0.00236)
Spell value growth	4.58e−05***	4.69e−05***	4.70e−05***
	(1.68e−05)	(1.67e−05)	(1.67e−05)
Multiple spell	0.754***	0.751***	0.751***
	(0.0169)	(0.0169)	(0.0169)
Gravity variables			
ln exporter GDP/cap	−0.0673***	−0.0638***	−0.0641***
	(0.00810)	(0.00821)	(0.00821)
ln importer GDP/cap	−0.0398***	−0.0485***	−0.0481***
	(0.00737)	(0.00748)	(0.00748)
Landlocked exporter	0.363***	0.353***	0.352***
	(0.0210)	(0.0210)	(0.0211)
Landlocked importer	−0.0464***	−0.0455***	−0.0462***
	(0.0162)	(0.0163)	(0.0163)
Common border	0.0178	0.0168	0.0165
	(0.0141)	(0.0142)	(0.0142)
Common language	0.102***	0.0981***	0.0980***
	(0.0121)	(0.0121)	(0.0121)
Common colonial past	0.141***	0.131***	0.132***
	(0.0198)	(0.0199)	(0.0199)
ln distance	0.0792***	0.0754***	0.0755***
	(0.00647)	(0.00654)	(0.00655)
Exchange-rate volatility	−0.000282**	−0.000311**	−0.000311**
	(4.34e−05)	(4.32e−05)	(4.32e−05)
Migration and product type variables			
Exporter migrants in importing country (EMIC)	−0.00480***	−0.00297**	−0.00303*
	(0.00144)	(0.00144)	(0.00175)
Importer migrants in exporting country	−0.00368**	−0.00239	−0.00250
	(0.00151)	(0.00155)	(0.00155)
EMIC*SSA		−0.0280***	−0.0252***
		(0.00340)	(0.00425)
Differentiated goods		−0.127***	−0.142***
		(0.0188)	(0.0398)
EMIC*Differentiated goods			9.05e−05
			(0.00217)
Differentiated goods*SSA			0.176*
			(0.0951)
EMIC*Differentiated goods *SSA			−0.00505
			(0.00562)
Observations	61,179	61,179	61,179
Exporting region FE (not reported)	yes	yes	yes
Importing region FE (not reported)	yes	yes	yes
Time effects (spell start year)	yes	yes	yes

Source: Authors.

Note: Robust standard errors in parentheses. FE = fixed effects; SSA = Sub-Saharan Africa.

Significance level: * = 10 percent, ** = 5 percent, *** = 1 percent.

importer country in the exporter one also has a negative effect in the first specification, which excludes interaction terms, but is insignificant in the other two specifications, shown in columns 2 and 3.

The second specification includes a dummy for differentiated goods as defined by Rauch (1999). The coefficient shows that differentiated goods tend to have longer spells (because the differentiated-goods dummy correlates negatively with hazard rates); this is consistent with the logic of the model in annex 1A of chapter 1, where larger sunk costs of entry raise the persistence of trade relationships. One may expect that the cost of searching for partners—and establishing trust—is higher for differentiated goods that vary, by construction, in terms of quality and attributes, than it is for homogeneous or reference-priced goods.

However, the interaction of the differentiated-goods variable with the stock of migrants from the exporting country in the importing one is insignificant, suggesting that diasporas do not significantly reduce search costs (otherwise they would reduce the survival of export spells, which would be reflected in a positive coefficient on the interaction term—here the coefficient is indeed positive but not significant).

As for Sub-Saharan Africa–specific effects, the higher survival observed for differentiated goods is weaker for African exports, suggesting that the type of differentiated goods exported from Africa may be less search-intensive.

Overall, this chapter shows how firm strategies and informal institutions have emerged to alleviate the information asymmetries (moral hazard and adverse selection) that plague cross-border transactions and often lead to premature, accidental terminations, which account for their low survival. These include the following:

- Geographical diversification, which helps firms hedge risks and access better inputs
- Self-enforcing contracts with credible non-legal sanctions, signaling, and reputations, which help alleviate moral hazard and adverse selection in the presence of incomplete contract enforcement
- Synergies (indirect spillovers) operating through cluster effects, which help alleviate credit rationing
- Migrant networks, which contribute to reduce moral hazard in trade relationships and overcome informational barriers.

These informal arrangements are even more critical to small-scale trade—largely unrecorded in statistics—which is a vital source of income to the poor and to vulnerable groups such as women traders. Providing an enabling environment for the development of such arrangements is key to ensuring that the gains from trade are inclusive and that the volatility of trade-related income is reduced through improved survival of trading relationships.

Whereas many, if not all, of these informal arrangements are market-driven, mediated through ethnic, national, or cultural networks, their efficacy can be encouraged by the right type of policies in terms of regulation, contract enforcement, banking supervision, and the provision of adequate information. In fact, the increasing evidence on the positive aspects of "learning from exporting" in developing countries suggests that programs that encourage the mentoring of potential exports by existing successful exporters in those countries and by firms in destination markets could be useful in increasing export survival rates.

Notes

1. In interpreting these results, it should be kept in mind that products in both studies are defined at very high levels of disaggregation, so adding one product does not mean a great deal of diversification.

2. Matching involves a two-step procedure to estimate the effect of a treatment that controls for selection into the treatment based on observable individual characteristics. In the first step, a probit is used to estimate the probability of being "treated" (here, the probability of being an exporting firm). The predicted probability of treatment, called a *propensity score*, is retrieved for use in the second stage. In the second stage, treated individuals (exporting firms) are matched with the controls (non-exporting firms) that have the closest propensity score (one or many, depending on the technique). The last stage of the procedure is to test whether the average performance outcome of treated firms (total factor productivity [TFP], capital intensity, and so on) significantly differs from that of matched control ones.

3. One should also keep in mind that the panels used in most of the studies cited, especially those from Sub-Saharan Africa, are very short in the time dimension, which does not help for the estimation of time-bound effects such as learning. Moreover, the matching differences-in-differences estimator used in most of the studies measures the impact effect of starting to export (that is, the matching differences compare the change in an outcome variable from the year before treatment to the treatment year, usually taken as the first year of export, between treated and control firms). It is unlikely that learning-by-exporting would have a traceable impact on performance outcomes within just one year.

4. Increased capital intensiveness may seem to be a puzzle, since African countries are unlikely to have a comparative advantage in capital-intensive goods. It should be kept in mind that these levels of capital intensiveness remain modest, with levels for control firms below the minimum level for efficient production of even labor-intensive products such as textiles and apparel. Higher capital intensity may also reflect the need for capital investment to satisfy more demanding standards in higher-income markets.

5. The data set was obtained directly from customs administrations in Ghana, Malawi, Senegal, and Tanzania as part of a World Bank research project.

6. Rajan and Zingales' measure of financial dependence is an industry-level variable calculated for 27 3-digit ISIC industries and 9 4-digit ones using Compustat data for the United States. Let k be capital expenditure and x be operational cash flow at the firm level. Rajan and Zingales' index for industry j, r_j, is the median value of $(k-x)/k$ across all Compustat firms in industry j. Index values, given in table 1 of Rajan-Zingales (1998), range from –45 for tobacco (ISIC 314) to 1.49 for drugs (ISIC 3522).

7. Braun proxies asset tangibility by the ratio of net property, plant, and equipment to market value at the firm level, using U.S. Compustat data. The industry-level variable is constructed, as in Rajan-Zingales, by taking the industry median at the ISIC 3-digit level. Index values, given in table 1 of Braun (2003), range from 0.09 (leather products) to 0.67 (petroleum refineries).

References

Albornoz, Facundo, H. F. Calvo Pardo, G. Corcos, and E. Ornelas. 2010. "Sequential Exporting." CEP Discussion Papers dp0974, Centre for Economic Performance, LSE.

Alvarez, Roberto, and H. Görg. 2009. "Multinationals and Plant Exit: Evidence from Chile." *International Review of Economics and Finance* 18: 45–51.

Alvarez, Roberto, and R. Lopez. 2005. "Exporting and Firm Performance: Evidence from Chilean Plants." *Canadian Journal of Economics* 38: 1384–400.

Araujo, Luis, and E. Ornelas. 2007. "Trust-Based Trade." Centre for Economic Performance (CEP) discussion paper 820.

Audretsch, David. 1991. "New Firm Survival and the Technological Regime." *Review of Economics and Statistics* 73: 520–26.

Audretsch, David, and T. Mahmood. 1995. "New-Firm Survival: New Results Using a Hazard Function." *Review of Economics and Statistics* 77: 97–103.

Audretsch, David, E. Santarelli, and M. Vivarelli. 1999. "Start-Up Size and Industrial Dynamics: Some Evidence from Italian Manufacturing." *International Journal of Industrial Organization* 17: 965–83.

Aw, Bee Yan, and A. R. Hwang. 1995. "Productivity in the Export Market: A Firm Level Analysis." *Journal of Development Economics* 47: 313–32.

Baldwin, John R., and W. Gu. 2003. "Export-Market Participation and Productivity Performance in Canadian Manufacturing." *Canadian Journal of Economics* 36: 634–57.

Bernard, Andrew B., J. Eaton, J. B. Jensen, and S. Kortum. 2003. "Plants and Productivity in International Trade." *American Economic Review* 93: 1268–90.

Bernard, Andrew B., and J. B. Jensen. 1995. "Exporters, Jobs, and Wages in U.S. Manufacturing: 1976-1987." *Brookings Papers on Economic Activity: Microeconomics* 67–119.

———. 1999. "Exceptional Exporter Performance: Cause, Effect, or Both?" *Journal of International Economics* 47: 1–25.

———. 2002. "The Deaths of Manufacturing Plants." NBER Working Paper 9026, National Bureau of Economic Research, Cambridge, MA.

———. 2004. "Why Some Firms Export." *Review of Economics and Statistics* 86 (2): 561–69.

———. 2007. "Firm Structure, Multinationals and Manufacturing Plant Deaths." *Review of Economics and Statistics* 89: 193–204.

Bernard, Andrew B., J. B. Jensen, S. Redding, and P. Schott. 2007. "Firms in International Trade." *Journal of Economic Perspectives* 21: 105–30.

Bernard, Andrew B., and F. Sjöholm. 2003. "Foreign Owners and Plant Survival." NBER Working Paper 10039, National Bureau of Economic Research, Cambridge, MA.

Bigsten, Arne, P. Collier, S. Dercon, M. Fafchamps, B. Gauthier, J. W. Gunning, A. Oduro, R. Oostendorp, C. Pattillo, M. Söderbom, F. Teal, and A. Zeuf. 2004. "Do African Manufacturing Firms Learn from Exporting?" *Journal of Development Studies* 40 (3): 115–41.

Bigsten, Arne, and M. Söderbom. 2006. "What Have We Learned from a Decade of Manufacturing Enterprise Surveys in Africa?" Policy Research Working Paper 3798, World Bank, Washington, DC.

Blalock, Garrick, and P. Gertler. 2004. "Learning from Exporting Revisited in a Less Developed Setting." *Journal of Development Economics* 75: 397–416.

Boermans, Martijn Adriaan. 2010. "Learning-by-Exporting and Destination Effects: Evidence from African SMEs." MPRA Paper 22658, University Library of Munich, Germany. Revised May 9, 2010.

Brambilla, Irene, D. Lederman, and G. Porto. 2010. "Exports, Export Destinations, and Skills." NBER Working Paper 15995, National Bureau of Economic Research, Cambridge, MA.

Braun, Mathias. 2003. "Financial Contractibility and Asset Hardness." Unpublished dissertation, Harvard University.

Cadot, Olivier, L. Iacovone, D. Pierola, and F. Rauch. 2011. "Success and Failure of African Exporters." Policy Research Working Paper 5657, World Bank, Washington, DC.

Carrère, Celine, and V. Strauss-Kahn. 2011 "Exports that Last: When Experience Matters." Unpublished document. ESCP Europe - CEPII.

Castellani, Davide. 2002. "Export Behavior and Productivity Growth: Evidence from Italian Manufacturing Firms." *Review of World Economics* 138: 605–28.

Clerides, Sofronis, S. Lach, and J. Tybout. 1998. "Is Learning by Exporting Import? Micro-Dynamic Evidence from Colombia." *Quarterly Journal of Economics* 113 (3): 903–47.

Cohen, Abner. 1971. "Cultural Strategies in the Organization of Trading Diasporas." In *The Development of Indigenous Trade and Markets in West Africa*, ed. C. Meillassoux, 266–78. London: Oxford University Press.

Collier, Paul, and J. W. Gunning. 1999. "Explaining African Economic Performance." *Journal of Economic Literature* 32: 64–111.

Crozet, Matthieu, K. Head, and T. Mayer. 2009. "Quality Sorting and Trade: Firm-Level Evidence for French Wine." CEPII Working Paper 2009-14, CEPII, Paris.

Damijan, Joze P., S. Polanec, and J. Prasnikar. 2004. "Self-Selection, Export Market, Heterogeneity and Productivity Improvements: Firm Level Evidence from Slovenia." LICOS Discussion Papers 14804, Katholieke Universiteit, Leuven.

De Loecker, Jan. 2004. "Do Exports Generate Higher Productivity? Evidence from Slovenia." LICOS Discussion Paper 151, Katholieke Universiteit, Leuven.

Delgado, Miguel A., J. Farinas, and S. Ruano. 2002. "Firm Productivity and Export Markets: A Non-Parametric Approach." *Journal of International Economics* 57: 397–422.

Disney, Richard, J. Haskel, and Y. Heden. 2003. "Entry, Exit and Establishment Survival in UK Manufacturing." *The Journal of Industrial Economics* 51: 91–112.

Doms, M., T. Dunne, and M. J. Roberts. 1995. "The Role of Technology Use in the Survival and Growth of Manufacturing Plants." *International Journal of Industrial Organization* 13: 523–42.

Dunne, T., M. J. Roberts, and L. Samuelson. 1988. "Patterns of Firm Entry and Exit in US Manufacturing Industries." *Rand Journal of Economics* 19: 495–515.

Eaton, Jonathan, M. Eslava, M. Kugler, and J. Tybout. 2008. "Export Dynamics in Colombia: Firm-Level Evidence." In *The Organization of Firms in a Global Economy*, ed. E. Helpman, D. Marin, and T. Verdier, 231–72. Cambridge, MA: Harvard University Press.

Ferragina, Anna, R. Pittiglio, and F. Reganati. 2011. "Multinational Status and Firm Exit in the Italian Manufacturing Sectors." Unpublished draft, University of Salerno.

Flamm, Kenneth. 1984. "The Volatility of Offshore Investment." *Journal of Development Economics* 16: 231–48.

Gereffi, Gary. 1999. "International Trade and Industrial Upgrading in the Apparel Commodity Chain." *Journal of International Economics* 48: 37–70.

Girma, Sourafel, and H. Görg. 2004. "Blessing or Curse? Domestic Plants Survival and Employment Prospects after Foreign Acquisition." *Applied Economics Quarterly* 50: 89–110.

Girma, Sourafel, D. Greenaway, and R. Kneller. 2004. "Does Exporting Increase Productivity? A Microeconometric Analysis of Matched Firms." *Review of International Economics* 12: 855–66.

Görg, Holger, and E. Strobl. 2003a. " 'Footloose' Multinationals?" *The Manchester School* 71 (1): 1–19.

———. 2003b. "Multinational Companies, Technology Spillovers and Plant Survival." *Scandinavian Journal of Economics* 105: 581–95.

———. 2004. "Foreign Direct Investment and Local Economic Development: Beyond Productivity Spillovers." Globalisation, Productivity and Technology Research Paper No. 2004/11. Available at SSRN: http://ssrn.com /abstract=715981 or http://dx.doi.org/10.2139/ssrn.715981.

Gould, David. 1994. "Immigrant Links to the Home Country: Empirical Implications for U.S. Bilateral Trade Flows." *Review of Economics and Statistics* 76: 302–16.

Graner, Mats, and A. Isaksson. 2007. "Firm Efficiency and the Destination of Exports: Evidence from Kenyan Plant-Level Data." Unpublished draft, UNIDO. http://www.unido.org/fileadmin/user_media/Publications/Pub_free /Firm_efficiency_and_destination_of_exports.pdf.

Greenaway, David, and R. Kneller. 2007. "Firm Heterogeneity, Exporting and Foreign Direct Investment." *The Economic Journal* 117: 134–61.

Greif, Avner. 1989. "Reputation and Coalitions in Medieval Trade: Evidence on the Maghribi Traders." *Journal of Economic History* 49: 857–82.

———. 1993. "Contract Enforceability and Economic Institutions in Early Trade: The Maghribi Traders' Coalition." *American Economic Review* 83: 525–48.

Hagemejer, Jan, and M. Kolasa. 2008. "Internationalization and Economic Performance of Enterprises: Evidence from Firm-Level Data." MPRA Working Paper 8720, Munich.

Hansson, Par, and N. Lundin. 2004. "Exports as Indicator on or as Promoter of Successful Swedish Manufacturing Firms in the 1990s." *Weltwirtschaftliches Archiv* 140, 415–445.

Harding, Alan, M. Söderbom, and F. Teal. 2004. "Survival and Success among African Manufacturers." CSAE Working Paper Series 2004–05, Centre for the Study of African Economies, University of Oxford.

Hausmann, Ricardo, and D. Rodrik. 2003. "Economic Development as Self-Discovery." *Journal of Development Economics* 72 (2): 603–33.

Head, Keith, and J. Ries. 1998. "Immigration and Trade Creation: Econometric Evidence from Canada." *Canadian Journal of Economics* 31: 47–62.

Isgut, Alberto. 2001. "What's Different about Exporters? Evidence from Colombian Manufacturing." *The Journal of Development Studies* 37 (5): 57–82.

Jaud, Mélise. 2011. "Food Safety, Reputation, and Trade." Working Paper halshs-00586310, HAL Paris School of Economics, Paris.

Kimura, F., and T. Fujii. 2003. "Globalizing Activities and the Rate of Survival: Panel Data Analysis on Japanese Firms." *Journal of Japanese International Economies* 17: 538–60.

Kimura, F., and K. Kiyota. 2006. "Exports, FDI and Productivity: Dynamic Evidence from Japanese Firms." *Review of World Economics* 142: 695–719.

Mata, J., and P. Portugal. 1994. "Life Duration of New Firms." *Journal of Industrial Economics* 42: 227–46.

———. 2002. "The Survival of New Domestic and Foreign-Owned Firms." *Strategic Management Journal* 23: 323–43.

Mayer, Thierry, M. Melitz, and G. Ottaviano. 2011. "Market Size, Competition, and the Product Mix of Exporters." Working Papers 2011-11, CEPII research center.

Melitz, Marc. 2003. "The Impact of Trade on Intra-Industry Reallocations and Aggregate Industry Productivity." *Econometrica* 71: 1695–725.

Mengistae, Taye, and C. Pattillo. 2004. "Export Orientation and Productivity in Sub-Saharan Africa." *IMF Staff Papers* 51 (2): 327–53.

Özler, Sule, and E. Taymaz. 2004. "Does Foreign Ownership Matter for Survival and Growth? Dynamics of Competition and Foreign Direct Investment." ERC Working Papers 0406, ERC (Economic Research Center), Middle East Technical University, Ankara, Turkey, revised March.

Pisu, Mauro. 2008. "Export Destinations and Learning-by-Exporting: Evidence from Belgium." NBB Working Paper 140, National Bank of Belgium, Brussels.

Rajan, Raghuram, and L. Zingales. 1998. "Financial Dependence and Growth." *American Economic Review* 88: 559–86.

Rankin, Neil, M. Söderbom, and F. Teal. 2006. "Exporting from Manufacturing Firms in Sub-Saharan Africa." *Journal of African Economies* 15: 671–87.

Ratha, Dilip, S. Mohapatra, C. Özden, S. Plaza, W. Shaw, and A. Shimeles. 2011. *Leveraging Migration for Africa: Remittances, Skills, and Investments.* Washington, DC: World Bank.

Rauch, James E. 1999. "Networks versus Markets in International Trade." *Journal of International Economics* 48 (1): 7–35.

———. 2001. "Business and Social Networks in International Trade." *Journal of Economic Literature* XXXIX, 1177–203.

Rauch, James E., and A. Casella. 2003. "Overcoming Informational Barriers to International Resource Allocation: Prices and Group Ties." *Economic Journal* 113: 21–42.

Rauch, James E., and V. Trindade. 2002. "Ethnic Chinese Networks in International Trade." *Review of Economics and Statistics* 84: 116–30.

Rauch, James E., and J. Watson. 2003. "Starting Small in an Unfamiliar Environment." *International Journal of Industrial Organization* 21: 1021–42.

Rhee, Yung-Whee, B. Ross-Larson, and G. Pursell. 1984. *Korea's Competitive Edge: Managing the Entry into World Markets.* Baltimore, MD: Johns Hopkins University Press.

Rodrik, Dani. 2000. "How Far Will International Economic Integration Go?" *Journal of Economic Perspectives* 14: 177–86.

Saxenian, AnnaLee. 1999. *Silicon Valley's New Immigrant Entrepreneurs.* San Francisco, CA: Public Policy Institute of California.

Taymaz, Erol, and S. Özler. 2007. "Foreign Ownership, Competition, and Survival Dynamics." *Review of Industrial Organization* 31 (1): 23–42.

Tewari, Meenu. 1999. "Successful Adjustment in Indian Industry: The Case of Ludhiana's Woolen Knitwear Industry." *World Development* 27: 1651–71.

Van Biesebroeck, Johannes. 2003. "Exporting Raises Productivity in Sub-Saharan Manufacturing Plants." NBER Working Paper 10020, National Bureau of Economic Research, Cambridge, MA.

Volpe, Christian, and J. Carballo. 2009. "Survival of New Exporters in Developing Countries: Does It Matter How They Diversify?" IDB working paper WP-I40, Inter-American Development Bank, Washington, DC.

Wagner, Joachim. 2002. "The Causal Effect of Exports on Firm Size and Labor Productivity: First Evidence from a Matching Approach." *Economics Letters* 77: 287–92.

———. 2007. "Exports and Productivity: A Survey of the Evidence from Firm-Level Data." *World Economy* 30: 60–82.

Weidenbaum, Murray, and S. Hughes. 1996. *The Bamboo Network.* New York, NY: The Free Press.

CHAPTER 4

Policy Implications

Improving the survival of African exports requires effort to make the environment in which African exporters operate friendlier through reduced trade costs and better upstream services, including, above all, better access to credit. These are standard prescriptions that would be reached by any study of African export performance, be it about entry, value, or survival, and are consistent with an agenda limiting the role of the government to setting clear rules, enforcing contracts, and providing base infrastructure.

This chapter will explore the question of whether there can be any role for more proactive policies. We will see that although preferential market access seems to have a limited role to play, any encouragement to trade with neighbors and regional trade may have far-reaching consequences for the ability of African firms to gradually build the capabilities that would allow them to serve more distant and more demanding markets, through gradual export-expansion paths.

However, we will also see that the very fragmentary evidence about the role of technical assistance in helping African firms cope with rising demands in terms of traceability and quality (in particular in agriculture) is ambiguous. More research is clearly needed to evaluate the impact of technical assistance, especially in view of the basic ambiguities of impact evaluation in this context.

Likewise, we will see that export promotion may have ambiguous effects on the sustainability of exports, possibly at times inducing exporters to spread themselves too thin. If export-promotion agencies are to contribute effectively to improve export sustainability, they probably need to include it as an explicit objective in the design and follow-up of assistance.

Thinking Strategically: Export-Expansion Paths

We saw in chapter 3 that the scale and scope on which firms export matter for survival at the product-origin-destination level (by *scale* we mean the number of destinations to which a product is shipped, and by *scope* we mean the number of products shipped to a given destination). However, these effects—at least as they are modeled in empirical papers—are essentially static and so do not tell a full story. In addition, they may well reflect omitted variables; for instance, scale may pick up the quality of a product, although quality may not be explicitly included as a separate variable. We now turn to dynamic effects—how to develop, grow, and survive.

The sequence in which exporters expand across foreign markets can make a difference to their survival prospects, according to findings by Carrère and Strauss-Kahn (2011). How much more sustainable are exports benefiting from prior product experience is shown in figure 4.1, which displays average first-year survival rates for product-origin cells on Organisation for Economic Co-operation and Development (OECD) markets (1) without prior extra-OECD experience (lower part of the bars) and (2) with one year of extra-OECD experience for the same product and origin. The effect is positive for exports originating from all regions (and significant, as these are regression results), but its magnitude varies substantially. For exports originating from East Asia and the Pacific, the first-year survival rate jumps by 11.6 percentage points, from 29.2 percent to 40.8 percent, a rise of over a third. For Sub-Saharan Africa, one year of experience outside the OECD raises the first-year survival rate by 7.4 percent—from 22 percent to 29.4 percent—a proportional increase of about one-third.

Carrère and Strauss-Kahn (2011) extend these first-pass results using Cox regressions with various controls, including gravity-type variables (distance, contiguity), initial values, origin-country income, and so on. Results confirm that one year of prior extra-OECD experience significantly enhances survival (in a broader sense than just first-year survival probabilities, since Cox regressions take into account hazard rates

Figure 4.1   Effect of Prior, Non-OECD Experience on First-Year Survival Rates by Region of Origin

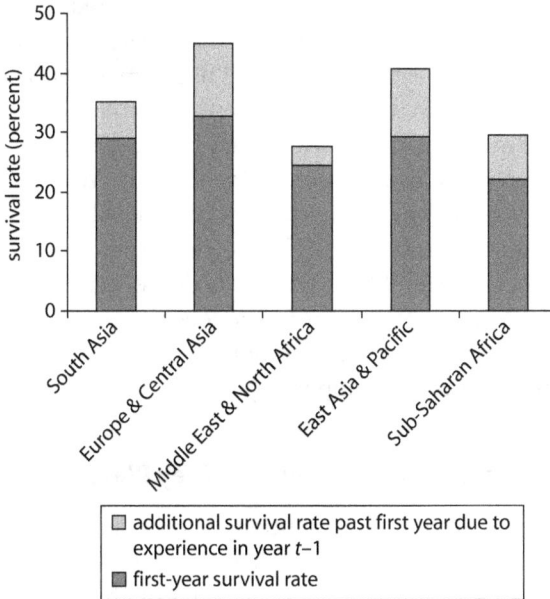

Source: Carrère and Strauss-Kahn 2011.

throughout a spell's life). A second year provides an additional boost, but the effect stops there, as additional years of prior experience have no significant effect on hazard rates.

In line with intuition, Carrère and Strauss-Kahn also find that experience effects are stronger for more differentiated products.[1] However, surprisingly, they find that a spell that has a destination market with imports of the same product from more origin countries lasts longer, as if tougher competition could be associated with longer survival. They interpret this as picking up unobservable market attractiveness effects; such effects could include more readily available and cheaper information on market access conditions and opportunities.

All in all, Carrère and Strauss-Kahn's analysis suggests that export-expansion strategies starting with Southern markets before targeting OECD ones may be a winning strategy. Experience in exporting to other developing countries can contribute to higher survival rates for firms when they subsequently enter OECD markets. Nevertheless, firms may get distracted from such a strategy by the large size of OECD markets and if the potential returns in those markets are higher than in neighboring developing countries. Even though we saw in chapter 3 that learning effects are limited when exporting to destination markets at similar incomes, there seems to be some learning not reflected in firm-level performance outcomes—total factor productivity, size, capital intensiveness, and so on—that helps later survival in OECD markets. These learning effects, which may be tacit knowledge, deserve further research. Also, one should keep in mind that these effects may be highly relevant for exporters who rely on their own resources for learning. When exporters get direct assistance from OECD buyers, they may be able to make the jump directly to demanding markets. This is clearly an area where export promotion programs should provide strategic assistance to exporters. In addition, the nature of a firms' prior experience of exporting should be an important indicator for export promotion agencies and donors when identifying priority firms to support.

Trade Preferences: What Role Should They Play?

Trade preferences, which have traditionally been an important factor in the landscape of African exports, can have many effects on their survival. Following the logic of the model in annex 1A of chapter 1, inasmuch as trade preferences reduce trade costs, they can be expected to reduce the incidence of exit decisions in the face of bad news and therefore to enhance survival. However, the empirical literature's results are ambiguous, suggesting, in particular, that selection and facilitating effects may work at cross-purposes.

In addition, Cadot, Olarreaga, and Tschopp (2009) showed that regional trade agreements have the effect of reducing the volatility of trade policy. They identified policy volatility as the absolute value of the year-on-year changes in the wedge between international and domestic prices, measured for agricultural products by the World Bank's agriculture distortions database (Anderson and Valenzuela, 2008).[2] They find that as countries sign more regional agreements—after controlling for the endogeneity of those agreements with instrumental-variable techniques—they have, all else being equal, lower policy volatility. Following again the logic of annex 1A of chapter 1, reducing the volatility of a key parameter of the exporter's profit function can have conflicting effects. On one hand, sudden policy or regulatory shifts can induce the premature termination of trade relationships. Reducing the frequency of such shifts on destination markets can contribute to better export survival. On the other hand, the volatility of export earnings encourages persistence through the good-news principle derived in annex 1A. Reducing this volatility may then dampen the positive effect of improved policy stability just outlined.

Which effect dominates is an empirical matter, and other effects can also be at play. Carrère and Strauss-Kahn (2011) explored empirically the effect of market access on export survival and found no positive effect. They introduced a market-access variable in a Cox regression of export survival estimated on a very large sample of 423,328 export spells from 165 non-OECD origin countries to OECD destinations over 47 years (1962–2010). These export spells came from 1,268 products at the very disaggregated Standard International Trade Classification (SITC) 5-digit level after eliminating raw materials and arms, left-censored spells, and trade flows of an annual value of less than US$1,000. The proxy is calculated at the origin-country level and is a GDP-weighted average of dummies for preferential access enjoyed by the origin country on any of its OECD destinations. After controlling for usual determinants of spell survival—see chapter 1—the market-access variable turns out to be correlated negatively with survival, as in Brenton, Pierola, and von Uexküll (2009).

This result may reflect the conflicting effects of reduced policy volatility outlined earlier. It may also reflect additional effects through which preferences may, somewhat paradoxically, *reduce* average export survival. Preferential trade agreements reduce the sunk costs of market entry and consequently—as documented empirically by Rakhman (2010)—raise the probability of entry. By reducing sunk costs, preferential market access can be expected to have two effects, *both going in the same direction*. First, lower sunk costs reduce the cost of entry and exit and can be expected to generate more churning in and out of partner export markets at the level of the firm (see, again, annex 1A of chapter 1). Second, easier entry may have a selection effect, inducing low-productivity firms to try their luck on the preferential market. As the distribution of exporting firms expands to the left—to low-productivity ones—it can be expected to generate more failures and therefore to reduce the aggregate survival probability.

However, it should be kept in mind that Carrère and Strauss-Kahn (2011) control for prior export experience, proxied by the existence of export spells of the same product originating from the same country. Thus, inasmuch as preferential agreements raise the likelihood of entry—which they do, according to Rakhman—they raise experience and therefore have an indirect positive effect on survival that is not picked up by the coefficient on the preferential-access proxy. In addition, Molina (2010) shows that the experience acquired in preferential trade is leveraged through entry on other markets as well. However, Molina does not explore whether the experience also translates into higher survival on those other markets.

Carrère and Strauss-Kahn also find that a larger number of countries exporting to a single destination reduces export survival at the cell (product-origin-destination) level. This suggests a crowding-out effect whereby different origin countries compete with each other in a given destination market, making the environment tougher. It stands in apparent contrast to the "crowding-in" effect identified at the firm level by Cadot et al. (2011) and discussed in chapter 1, although the crowding-in or synergy effect in question was between producers from the same origin country, not across origin countries. The mechanisms suggested by these authors to explain the synergy effect are unlikely to play *between* origin countries.

All in all, it is fair to say that the recent evidence on the effect of trade preferences on survival is ambiguous, reflecting multiple channels of influence. On one hand, trade preferences (1) reduce trade costs and (2) generate experience, both of which can be expected to enhance survival. On the other hand, they reduce *entry* costs, which may be expected to reduce survival through both (1) a more severe reaction to random fluctuations in profitability and (2) a selection effect that draws in weaker players. If these forces balance each other, trade preferences are unlikely to have a strong effect, either way, on export survival. This tentative—and qualitative—conclusion is consistent with the casual observation that African exporters have had preferential access to many OECD markets for several decades now and have, nevertheless, not shown particular resilience. However, this may also reflect weaknesses in the particular preference programs whereby products that are sensitive in OECD countries—often those with the largest preference margins—are excluded from the scheme or are subject to restrictive rules of origin. Thus, the number of products included with rules of origin that are not a major constraint may be small and the preference margins may not be sufficient to offset the costs of an adverse trade and business climate.

A Role for Support Services and Technical Assistance

Policies can take forms other than trade preferences. In this section we consider the role that technical assistance and other forms of support can play in promoting the survival of exports.

Upstream Services and Export Survival

Export performance is the product of managerial capabilities and firm resources, which include access to quality inputs. This was illustrated recently in a paper by Ferro, Portugal-Perez, and Wilson (2011), who showed that aid for trade directed at service sectors—including transport, information and communication technologies, energy, banking, and business—raised the export performance of downstream manufacturing sectors. While ostensibly aimed at overcoming reverse-causality problems in the estimation of aid effectiveness, those authors' identification strategy uncovered an interesting causal chain from upstream services to downstream export performance in manufacturing sectors.

Can we similarly link the performance of upstream service sectors to the ability of downstream exporters to survive in foreign markets? Jaud and Kukenova (2011) show that the answer is "yes." Their paper highlights the low level of access to credit in Africa, with credit/GDP ratios about five times lower in Africa than in OECD countries. Indeed, we saw in chapter 3 that access to finance was highlighted as the single most important constraint reported by African exporters in the recent World Bank survey. In particular, 47 percent of past (failed) exporters cited lack of access to finance as a major constraint. We also saw, in chapter 2, that the importance of access to credit is likely to rise as agricultural exporters are forced to comply with increasingly stringent standards and technical regulations.

In order to identify how improvements in the functioning of credit markets contribute to overcome the high infant mortality of African agri-food exports, Jaud and Kukenova rely on a measure of dependence on finance at the product level. Specifically, they use a measure of the riskiness of products in terms of their probability of being rejected at the European Union (EU) border for sanitary reasons (see box 4.1).

The policy hypothesis tested by Jaud and Kukenova is that financial development improves disproportionately the sustainability of "risky" exports, because those products are likely to be particularly dependent on credit, whether in order to invest in quality upgrading or to weather sudden crises, such as bans or product rejections. They do this by regressing the hazard rate of African agri-food exports on the EU market using a Cox regression on the product riskiness index, the level of financial development of the origin country, and an interaction term between the two. Their working hypothesis suggests that the interaction term should be negative, indicating a reduction in hazard rates for risky products over and above the general effect that financial development has on the survival of all exports.

Box 4.1

The Agri-Food Product Risk Index

The agri-food product risk index measures the product's ability to comply with EU agri-food standards and technical regulations. Put differently, this index measures the gap between mandated and actual quality. It is constructed from a database of EU food alerts as reported in the Rapid Alert System for Food and Feed (RASFF) at the Harmonized System (HS)-8 level of disaggregation. A naïve count of food alerts at the EU border might correlate with riskiness as defined above (a higher count of alerts meaning a riskier product), but such an assessment would be confounded by many influences, including the quality of sanitary controls in the origin country and possibly hidden protectionist motives at the EU border. In order to filter out these confounding influences, Cadot, Jaud, and Suwa (2012) ran a regression of the count alerts at the (product × exporter) level during the RASFF's eight years of records (2000–08) on the past occurrence of bans, import shares on the EU market, and proxies for protectionist motives (for example, quotas or World Trade Organization disputes). Product fixed effects were then retrieved from the regression, providing unbiased estimates of the propensity of products to be stopped at the EU border.

"Risky" products are defined by positive fixed effects. These high-propensity products are characterized by a large gap between EU standards and what is currently offered by exporters to the European Union; these products are therefore likely to require substantial investments in quality control. Alternatively, exporters of such products may expect periodic disruptions caused by alerts and shipment rejections.

Source: Cadot, Jaud, and Suwa 2012.

Their estimation exercise uses a firm-level data set already used in chapter 2 for four African countries—Ghana, Mali, Senegal, and Tanzania—compiled by the World Bank from customs transaction-level records. Their base index of financial development is the credit/GDP ratio taken from Beck, Demirgüç-Kunt, and Levine (2000). They find that, indeed, whereas financial development has, on average, a negative and significant effect on export hazard rates for all products and countries in the sample, the effect is reinforced by the interaction term with product riskiness, which is also negative and significant. In order to get a feel for the magnitudes involved, we note that in 2003 Senegal's financial development—as proxied by its credit/GDP ratio—was about three times that of Tanzania. If the latter were to reach the former's level of financial development, the hazard rate for shrimp exports—a highly risky product as measured by the riskiness index—would go down by 7 percent for Tanzania. That is, the probability of surviving one more year would go up by roughly 7 percent. Depending on the initial hazard rate, this could be a very substantial increase in the survival probability. For instance, with an initial hazard rate of 0.7, the survival rate would jump by 16 percent, from 0.30 to 0.35.

Our discussion of the role of technical regulations and standards in chapter 2, in particular in agro-food products, highlighted their potential to disrupt trade flows through sudden regulatory changes or through the arbitrary application of regulations at the border. U.S. food safety regulations, in particular, explicitly allow for discretionary and informal "profiling" in the application of regulations at the border (see Jouanjean, Maur, and Shepherd 2011).

Technical Assistance: Does It Help?

In chapter 3 of this report we discussed how the administration of sanitary and phytosanitary (SPS) measures could be a factor in the low survival for African agri-food exports. Recognizing this, the European Union has put in place programs designed to help producers in low-income countries, in particular African, Caribbean, and Pacific (ACP) countries,[3] to cope with those measures. If well designed, such programs have the potential of helping to secure market access for producers who would otherwise have difficulty following, and complying with, the rising tide of sanitary and technical regulations in their EU markets.

Recent research by Jaud and Cadot (2011) suggests that, when subjected to rigorous impact evaluation, technical assistance programs may turn out to have less of an impact than expected, as treatment-effect methodologies uncover no significant performance improvement for "treated" firms. In this section, we consider a similar exercise using export survival—rather than export growth—as the performance measure, and find similarly insignificant treatment effects. However, impact-evaluation results should be interpreted very cautiously, for reasons that we will discuss later on in this section.

Jaud and Cadot focused on the Pesticide Initiative Program (PIP). Financed by the European Development Fund (EDF) with an overall budget of 34.1 million euros, the PIP started in 2001, initially for a five-year period; it was extended by two additional years, and a new wave was launched in 2009 following a positive evaluation of the program's first phase.

The PIP has two main objectives. The first is to enable ACP exporters of fresh fruit and vegetables (FFV) to comply with European traceability and food safety requirements (in particular as regards pesticide residues). The second is to consolidate the position of small-scale producers in the ACP horticultural value chain. Support activities are organized around five components: (1) good company practices, (2) training, (3) capacity building, (4) regulation and standards, and (5) information and communication.

The core of the support (almost 30 percent of the program's budget) goes to component 1, which consists of helping producers and exporters to set up internal food safety management systems in production and marketing operations. The regulation and standards component ensures that all substances recommended in crop protocols ("technical itineraries") are authorized in both the European Union and the origin country. Finally, the capacity-building component aims at developing national capacity to provide the services needed by the industry. Beneficiaries of capacity-building activities include private consultants (training courses on food safety, pesticide use, and integrated pest management [IPM]); accredited laboratories (pesticide residue analysis); public services (including extension services and pesticide registration bodies); and strong professional organizations.

Eligibility starts with the completion and submission of a request for PIP intervention addressing the applicant's particular needs and objectives. The request identifies by self-assessment the problem to be resolved—for example, maximum residue levels (MRLs), non-accredited plant-protection products, or traceability—and puts forward possible fixes such as training in integrated crop management (ICM)/IPM systems or the safe use of pesticides, implementation of food safety and traceability systems, or "technical itineraries." To be accepted, a requested intervention must help to achieve product compliance with EU traceability and food safety (pesticide residues) regulations. Upon acceptance, a protocol stating the actions to be implemented by each party on a cost-sharing basis (50 percent for each, except for smallholders who are expected to contribute only 20 percent) is signed. The actions listed in the protocol are chosen from among a menu offered by PIP under its five components; however, the combination in each protocol is specific to a firm and varies across beneficiaries.

So far, most of the financing has gone to training costs, technical support and the development of a food safety toolbox containing crop protocols, good agricultural practice (GAP) guidelines, and Hortitrace, a traceability software developed by PIP. The program's first phase has covered 21 countries,[4] along with 320 export companies. Out of those, 219 firms benefited from the "good company practices" component (advice and assistance for setting up sanitary quality and traceability systems, and certification pre-audits), and 153 benefited from training under the capacity-building component.

An evaluation of PIP's first phase was undertaken in June 2008. Overall, the evaluation report drew up a very positive image of the program's impact, contributing to the launch of a second five-year phase in 2009. However, although fairly comprehensive, PIP's evaluation suffers from a typical drawback of this type of exercise—namely, the lack of a counterfactual to benchmark the performance of treated firms and products. Like many technical assistance programs, PIP has never been subjected to a rigorous impact evaluation. As part of a World Bank work program on impact evaluation, Jaud and Cadot (2011) used a combination of customs and program data to assess, using difference-in-difference (DID) regression with propensity-score matching if PIP had an impact on the export performance of beneficiary firms, relative to nonbeneficiary (control) ones. The comparison with a control group is crucial in the case of Senegal's FFV exports, because the whole industry underwent a boom starting in 2000–01, at the same time PIP was launched. If the performance of beneficiary (treatment) firms was compared only with their own performance prior to the treatment, the estimated treatment effect would be very large. However, this estimated effect could also reflect many factors other than the treatment. Only a comparison of the performance of treated and control firms over the same time period can filter out confounding influences common to all firms. Using this technique, Jaud and Cadot found no significant impact.

For this report, we ran DID regressions similar in spirit to those in Jaud and Cadot, but instead of considering export growth as the outcome (performance) variable, we used their survival, using Cox regressions. Results are shown in table 4.1. The regressions control for several firm attributes (initial sales, employment, and number of FFV products) as well as destination effects. The unit of observation is a firm-product-destination combination.

Table 4.1   Cox Regression Results: The PIP Effect on Survival of Senegalese FFV Exports to the EU Market

	(1)	(2)	(3)	(4)	(5)	(6)
Treatment variable	0.221	−0.467	−0.314	−0.225	0.213	−0.244
	(0.74)	(1.48)	(0.75)	(0.63)	(0.53)	(0.70)
Destination effects						
Germany	0.349	0.456	0.755	0.766	0.886	0.704
	(1.11)	(1.47)	(2.58)***	(2.53)**	(2.10)**	(1.90)*
Spain	0.423	0.681	0.443	0.380	0.306	0.189
	(1.77)*	(1.80)*	(1.26)	(1.26)	(0.77)	(0.60)
France	−0.336	−0.512	−0.589	−0.588	−0.192	−0.209
	(2.02)**	(2.00)**	(1.75)*	(1.71)*	(0.59)	(0.57)
United Kingdom	0.472	0.436	0.414	0.346	0.889	0.964
	(1.05)	(0.91)	(0.88)	(0.71)	(2.52)**	(2.98)***
Italy	−0.138	0.103	0.738	0.779	1.053	0.842
	(0.37)	(0.20)	(1.40)	(1.40)	(2.97)***	(3.09)***
Netherlands	0.321	0.140	−0.032	−0.034	0.352	0.385
	(1.72)*	(0.38)	(0.10)	(0.09)	(0.97)	(1.07)
Firm attributes						
Initial sales		−0.218		−0.675	−0.273	−0.658
		(0.83)		(0.69)	(0.38)	(0.68)
Initial employment			−0.092	0.495	0.462	−0.075
			(0.39)	(0.50)	(0.60)	(0.10)
Initial export growth					−0.366	−0.498
					(3.58)***	(5.32)***
Log natural of FFV products						1.305
						(3.31)***

Source: Authors.
Note: FFV = fresh fruit and vegetables. Dependent variable: robust z-statistics in parentheses.
Significance level: * = 10 percent, ** = 5 percent, *** = 1 percent.

The regressions show significant destination effects, with hazard rates significantly higher (than in countries not shown on the list, the omitted category) on the German market and lower on the French market. But—and this is the important finding for this report—they show no significant effect of the treatment.

These results, which are based on a single impact evaluation, have no claim to external validity. In addition, the absence of treatment effects should be interpreted very cautiously, and the caveats may actually be more important than the result itself.

On one hand, the absence of treatment effects may reflect program ineffectiveness, in which case the impact evaluation says what it is meant to say. On the other hand, the absence of treatment effect may reflect the presence of externalities. Externalities are involved when technical assistance programs include changes in managerial or technical practices by beneficiary firms that are easily imitated by other firms. Unless the control group can exclude "imitator" firms, its performance will be affected (positively) by the treatment, thus reducing the performance differential between the treatment and control groups—that is, the treatment effect. Thus, for a given true value of the treatment effect, the stronger the externality, the weaker the value of the *estimated* treatment effect.

The bias introduced by externalities in the measurement of treatment effects is a crucial issue because externalities provide the ultimate justification for government intervention—if all the treatment's benefits were internalized by beneficiary firms, the treatment could be provided by the private sector without the need for public funds. Thus, how to interpret the absence of the estimated treatment effect depends on the underlying externality.

To see this, consider two alternative sources of market failures. In the first case, improved practices are easily imitable, and hence investment in upgraded practices is not appropriable. In other words, firms will not invest in upgrading practices because they can wait to imitate others. Let us call this case *no-appropriability*. In the second case, practices can be improved only upon a large investment in knowledge production that involves indivisibilities and no "rivalry" (zero marginal cost), such as inviting foreign experts to give a one-week training course. However, these practices are not observable or imitable by other firms, so there is no appropriability issue. In that case, no individual firm has the resources to undertake the investment because it is too large, but a coordinating mechanism, such as a government program, may work.

Suppose that a government program has been implemented in each case, and consider the interpretation of either significant or insignificant treatment effects. In the first case (non-appropriability), a significant treatment effect means that the program was successful, but that beneficiaries managed to internalize the benefits. Then it must be the case that the non-appropriability problem in fact does not exist, so the market could (at least in principle) be relied on to provide the training. By contrast, a non-significant effect can be either good news or bad news: it may mean that the treatment worked but that there was indeed a problem of appropriability, in which case it would be justified; or, simply, that it failed. In the second case (where investment is too large and knowledge cannot be imitated), a significant treatment effect is consistent with the existence of the market failure. This is unambiguously good news, and the opposite is true if the treatment effect is insignificant. Thus, estimated treatment effects provide unambiguous policy signals only when the externality is of the second type.[5]

What are we left with? First, there is a serious knowledge gap concerning the effectiveness of technical assistance programs. Most technical assistance program-evaluation designs are content with satisfaction surveys, which are subject to many biases. Programs should be readied for rigorous impact evaluation at the design stage. Only with the accumulation of impact evaluation results will we know if the programs actually have an effect or not. Second, the estimation of treatment effects should be, whenever possible, complemented by an attempt to estimate the strength of externalities. Cadot et al. (2012) provide an example, which is discussed in the section below. Third, beyond impact effects (the usual focus of DID estimation), sustainability should be an area of focus for impact evaluation, because sustainability is a second area where knowledge gaps are very large. Last but not least, anecdotal evidence highlights the importance of managerial factors in the viability of export relationships. For instance, Egan and Mody (1992) relate:

> Buyers looking for either new sources of supply or joint venture partners search for suppliers who manage their factories efficiently, often regardless of the level of technology those factories currently employ; interviewees commonly felt that new machines could easily be installed so long as workers already had the ability to use them efficiently and absorb training readily. For many buyers, management was the most important factor in defining an ideal supplier. . . . As one buyer phrased it, "I do not invest in plant X but in Mr Y. it all depends on the people" (Egan and Mody 1992, p. 326, quoted in Rauch and Watson 2003).

Thus, useful technical assistance programs should emphasize managerial training as much as technology—in accordance, incidentally, with the buyers' rising emphasis on quality and traceability, which have strong implications for management structure within the firm and along the entire supply chain. Thus, there may be a useful role for government to encourage and facilitate successful exporters in the country to share their knowledge and experiences with potential exporters. A further role would be that of setting up a mentoring scheme whereby successful exporters—at home or overseas—support nascent exporters in poor African countries.

Export Promotion

Widely used around the world, export-promotion agencies have been set up essentially to help inexperienced exporters to establish initial contacts abroad or to expand from a narrow base. Recent evidence (see Lederman, Olarreaga, and Payton 2009) suggests that these agencies have been, by and large, fairly successful in that regard, at least provided some key conditions—such as private sector involvement in their management structure—were met. But can export-promotion agencies help improve export sustainability?

Recent evidence from an impact evaluation of Tunisia's export-promotion scheme, FAMEX, suggests that sustainability may precisely be the program's Achilles heel. Using matching-DID estimation on a data set that combines firm-level export performance from customs with program data, Cadot et al. (2012) show that the program's effect typically vanishes after two years. This does not mean that the trade relationships it generated were interrupted, however: the treatment effect on the number of products and destinations served by the beneficiary firms is more persistent than its effect on monetary export values. What the finding suggests is that beneficiaries may have tended to spread themselves too thin.

This conjecture is confirmed by the observation that treated firms took a beating at the outset of the global financial crisis, in 2009, compared with control firms. Indeed, even though treated firms were more diversified than control firms after the treatment—as measured by the Herfindahl or Theil indexes on product-destination cells—they face no less price risk in their overall export portfolio, suggesting that their marginal products and destinations were either heavily correlated with existing ones in terms of price risk, or even riskier.[6]

If one follows the logic of Rauch and Watson (2003), by increasing the ease of matching, successful export promotion may even reduce—albeit indirectly—the persistence of trade relationships (because it reduces sunk costs of entry and exit in particular trade relationships). However, even if it makes particular trade relationships less persistent, it may make aggregate ones more persistent, as firms shift more easily across partners but within a product-destination cell.

Thus, improving the contribution of export promotion to the sustainability of exports may involve some additional emphasis on the long-term sustainability of the trade relationships. This may involve, first, additional criteria, such as consistency with comparative advantage (see chapter 2), or adequacy of the match in terms of firm size. To quote Tewari,

From a policy perspective [...] it may be more fruitful for development agencies to encourage small and medium-sized local firms that are first-time exporters to develop relationships with medium-sized overseas buyers, rather than merely go for large retail chains. The latter may work better for more experienced or already established exporters (Tewari 1999, p. 1664).

It may also involve stronger follow-up and long-term technical assistance to accompany the firm's technology and management upgrading.

The previous chapter also discussed how diasporas can overcome some of the constraints that undermine export survival. However, export promotion agencies have in general done little to work with and encourage links between exporters and the diasporas, especially within Africa. One important opportunity comes from using overseas diplomatic missions to support export promotion efforts by helping to link exporting firms to diasporas.

Notes

1. Carrère and Strauss-Kahn measure product differentiation by the size of the cross-country elasticity of substitution as measured by Broda and Weinstein (2006).

2. The World Bank's Agricultural Distortions Database is available at www .worldbank.org/agdistortions.

3. ACP countries have enjoyed long-standing preferential access to EU markets, first through the Lome Convention, then through the Cotonou Convention, and finally through a set of Economic Partnership Agreements currently under negotiation.

4. Benin, Burkina Faso, Cameroon, Côte d'Ivoire, the Dominican Republic, Gambia, Ghana, Guinea, Jamaica, Kenya, Mali, Mauritius, Mozambique, Namibia, Senegal, Surinam, Tanzania, Togo, Uganda, Zambia, and Zimbabwe.

5. We are grateful to Daniel Lederman for helping us to clarify this point.

6. Cadot et al.'s measure of price risk was constructed as follows. Consider a Tunisian firm selling men's cotton t-shirts in Germany. The import unit values of all men's cotton t-shirts imported into Germany from origins other than Tunisia were aggregated into an import-weighted average price, which was tracked over the entire sample period. This calculation was repeated for all of the firm's active product-destination cells. Then, a scaled measure of the portfolio's risk was generated out of the 10-year variances and covariances of the average unit values of all those cells. That scaled risk measure is the coefficient of variation of the entire export portfolio. As the firm shifts its portfolio over

time (for instance, as a result of FAMEX assistance), the risk measure shifts under a pure composition effect (shifting cell shares). The risk measure was then introduced in the matching-DID estimation as an outcome measure. The treatment effect was found insignificant, meaning that treated firms, in spite of their reduced concentration, failed to reduce the price risk to which they were exposed.

References

Anderson, Kym, and E. Valenzuela. 2008. "Estimates of Global Distortions to Agricultural Incentives, 1955 to 2007." World Bank, Washington, DC.

Beck, Thorsten, A. Demirgüç-Kunt, and R. Levine. 2000. "A New Database on Financial Development and Structure." *World Bank Economic Review* 14: 597–605.

Brenton, Paul, M. D. Pierola, and E. von Uexküll. 2009. "The Life and Death of Trade Flows: Understanding the Survival Rates of Developing-Country Exporters." In *Breaking into New Markets: Emerging Lessons for Export Diversification*, ed. R. Newfarmer, W. Shaw, and P. Walkenhorst, 127–44. Washington, DC: World Bank.

Brenton, Paul, C. Saborowski, and E. von Uexküll. 2011. "What Explains the Low Survival Rate of Developing Country Export Flows." *The World Bank Economic Review* 24: 474–99.

Broda, Christian, and D. E. Weinstein. 2006. "Globalization and the Gains from Variety." *The Quarterly Journal of Economics*, MIT Press 121 (2): 541–85, May.

Cadot, Olivier, A. Fernandes, J. Gourdon, and A. Mattoo. 2012. "Are Export Support Programs Effective? Evidence from Tunisia." Unpublished draft, World Bank, Washington, DC.

Cadot, Olivier, L. Iacovone, D. Pierola, and F. Rauch. 2011. "Success and Failure of African Exporters." Policy Research Working Paper 5657, World Bank, Washington, DC.

Cadot, Olivier, M. Jaud, and A. Suwa. 2012. "Do Food Scares Explain Supplier Concentration? An Analysis of EU Agri-Food Imports." In *Non-Tariff Measures: A Fresh Look at Trade Policy's New Frontier*, ed. O. Cadot and M. Malouche, Washington, DC and London: World Bank and CEPR.

Cadot, Olivier, M. Olarreaga, and J. Tschopp. 2009. "Does Regionalism Reduce Trade-Policy Volatility?" Agricultural Distortions Working Paper 88, World Bank, Washington, DC.

Carrère, Céline, and V. Strauss-Kahn. 2011. "Exports that Last: When Experience Matters." Draft, University of Geneva.

Egan, M. L., and A. Mody. 1992. "Buyer-Seller Links in Export Development." *World Development* 20: 321–34.

Ferro, Esteban, A. Portugal-Perez, and J. Wilson. 2011. "Aid for Trade and Export Performance: The Case of Aid in Services." In *Where to Spend the Next Million? Applying Impact Evaluation to Trade Assistance*, O. Cadot, A. Fernandes, J. Gourdon, and A. Mattoo, 207–19. Washington, DC and London: World Bank and CEPR.

Jaud, Mélise, and O. Cadot. 2011. "A Second Look at the Pesticides Initiative Program: Evidence from Senegal." Policy Research Working Paper 5635, World Bank, Washington, DC.

Jaud, Mélise, and M. Kukenova. 2011. "Financial Development and the Survival of African Agri-food Exports." Policy Research Working Paper 5649, World Bank, Washington, DC.

Jouanjean, Marie-Agnes, J.-C. Maur, and B. Shepherd. "US SPS Enforcement: Do Refusals Harm Reputation?" Forthcoming in *Non-Tariff Measures: New Analysis for Trade Policy's New Frontier*, ed. O. Cadot and M. Malouche. London/Washington, DC: The World Bank and CEPR (Center for Economic and Policy Research).

Lederman, Daniel, M. Olarreaga, and L. Payton. 2009. "Export Promotion Agencies Revisited." Policy Research Working Paper 5125. World Bank, Washington, DC.

Molina, Ana-Cristina. 2010. "Are Preferential Agreements Stepping Stones to Other Markets?" Graduate Institute of International and Development Studies Working Paper 13-2010, Geneva.

Rakhman, Anna. 2010. "Export Duration and New Market Entry." Unpublished draft, George Washington University, Washington, DC.

Rauch, James E., and J. Watson. 2003. "Starting Small in an Unfamiliar Environment." *International Journal of Industrial Organization* 21: 1021–42.

Tewari, Meenu. 1999. "Successful Adjustment in Indian Industry: The Case of Ludhiana's Woolen Knitwear Industry." *World Development* 27: 1651–71.

www.ingramcontent.com/pod-product-compliance
Lightning Source LLC
Chambersburg PA
CBHW070406200326
41518CB00011B/2087